Advanced Money

Planning Investments
on Your Computer

Advanced Money

Planning Investments on Your Computer

Charles Seiter and Steven Nichols

Addison-Wesley Publishing Company, Inc.
Reading, Massachusetts   Menlo Park, California
Don Mills, Ontario   Wokingham, England   Amsterdam
Sydney   Singapore   Tokyo   Mexico City   Bogota
Santiago   San Juan

Library of Congress Cataloging in Publication Data

Seiter, Charles.
  Advanced money.

  Includes index.
  1. Investments—Data processing. 2. Finance,
Personal—Data processing. I. Nichols, Steven.
II. Title.
HG4515.5.S45 1985   332.6'028'54 84-24529
ISBN 0-201-06598-3

Cover design by Marshall Henrichs. Text design by Lori Snell.
Set in 11-point Aster by Kingsport Press.

ISBN 0-201-06598-3

ABCDEFGHIJ-DO-8765
First printing, January 1985

Contents

Advanced Money

Planning Investments
on Your Computer

INTRODUCTION
A Letter to the Reader

The development of more and more powerful computers for personal use has proceeded at a truly breathtaking pace. In 1975, the mere existence of personal computers seemed miraculous. By 1980, however, the earliest computers had begun to seem quaint (one of the authors for a short time sold an interesting kit from the antique era, the Apple I—there really was one!). By 1984, machines that would have seemed faintly like science fiction in 1980—the Macintosh, for example—were available.

There is no doubt that people are better at thinking up amazing hardware than at figuring out what to do with it. If this statement appears somewhat harsh, try this experiment: hook up a video recorder to a lovely new 25-inch perfect-picture color TV and record three random hours of weeknight television. Then watch the tape ten times in a row and at the end of this ordeal decide for yourself whether the machinery is of higher quality than the programming.

Much the same situation exists in computer software, now that computers are virtually as widespread as TVs. Extremely competent word-processing software has arisen, because this is a well-focused application with great demand. Furthermore, it appears as if the world of business was just waiting for spreadsheet-calculation software. Beyond these areas, however, things get somewhat fuzzy, and there seems to be little consensus on just what kinds of software—in particular, financial software—personal-computer users need. This confusion has called forth a great number of two-hundred-dollar, disk-based wonder packages, many of which are completely irrelevant to anyone's needs.

For example, ads for systems that purportedly keep track

of your stock portfolio typically do not dwell on the problem that you yourself must enter all the information concerning the stocks. One package boasts that it ". . . notifies you the day your profits become long-term capital gains!" Well, it will if you happen to have any profits and have also updated your disk file on that date; but you should know that anyone who can operate a calendar could obtain that information when the stock is purchased.

In most of these personal finance systems, beyond the usual loan payment calculations there is really only computerized record-keeping, which is more trouble than it is worth if your holdings are less than vast. It is not clear that anyone has really benefited from the possibility of computer recipe files (do you want hot oil splattered on your IBM PC?), and it is also not clear that anyone needs a disk file, which must be updated daily, to follow the course of three or four stocks. Paper is ideal for these applications and doesn't lose data when bent, heated, or passed near a magnet.

This book grows out of some strong beliefs about what computers should do for you. The premise here is that the computer can help you make specific decisions about specific situations involving money. It can't really help you predict stock prices, for example, because there is little evidence that anyone knows how to write a program that will do that consistently. And if you have a difficult time keeping track of your checkbook, you probably just need a calculator and a little more attention to your carefree ways. Many of the computations involved in comparing investment possibilities are just poisonously tiresome, however, and this is exactly where the computer becomes useful. The programs here have two characteristics:

- They are short—short enough that they are easy to type in and save and short enough that they can be completely explained. The idea is that nothing should be "left to the experts"; *you* should understand, in detail, what is going on with your own money. In every complex piece of software, the danger exists that the computer will seem to be giving its electronic blessing to different courses of action. All a computer can do is make calculations based on different assumptions implicit in the programming—if the assumptions are inaccurate the computer will dutifully crank out misleading nonsense.

- They are specific. Most people will find that handling their savings reduces to a fairly small set of opportunities and that their investment decisions are quite concrete, for example, money market vs. mutual fund or rent/buy stocks vs. buy a house. Although it is standard advice in this business not to put all your eggs in one basket, the reality is that middle-class families in America are going to have to make hard choices, and make them correctly, about a small number of eggs and at most a few baskets. If by chance you are one of the lucky few with more than $120,000 a year to invest, here's some gratuitous advice derived from the career of the economist John Maynard Keynes. Lord Keynes, by any criteria one of the most successful investors and influential thinkers of this century, was asked on his deathbed if he had any regrets, and he answered that he thought he should have drunk more champagne. As of the mid-1980s, Dom Perignon is selling at sensational bargain prices because of the franc's decline against the dollar. Get the picture?

The hope of the authors is that this book will help you get some feeling for the possible uses of your money and will help you formulate your own strategy for protecting and improving your financial position. Along the way, you will probably pick up a little bit of BASIC programming experience and develop some intuition about different kinds of investment situations. Examining a variety of examples usually makes a stronger impression on people than examining a theoretical treatment, and, take our word for it, you will get to see all sorts of examples that you would rather see on a computer screen than in a bank statement.

1

Two Grand Ahead of the Game

Given that you are old enough to be reading this book and that you are probably imaginative enough to have bought a computer, it cannot have escaped your attention that a reasonable shorthand description of at least one fundamental principle of economics is "Them that has, gits." Unlike various other folksy maxims, such as "Never rains but it pours" and "Don't play poker with a man called Doc," this one has been thoughtfully quantified for your edification by a variety of lending institutions. As we review the evidence, please try not to be discouraged if you find yourself on the wrong side of the numbers; help, at least in the form of copious encouragement and advice, is on its way even in this very chapter.

In the peppy financial market of the mid-1980s, you can walk into almost any bank or savings and loan and ask to see a rate card, which looks something like a menu and outlines what your savings options are, for different lengths of time and different amounts of money. One column will tell you, for example, what interest rates are available for 90-day certificates.

Table 1A shows some actual figures, from mid-1983, from a bank that shall remain anonymous but that would doubtless not be embarrassed anyway. Looking over this table as a small saver, consider what these numbers mean. The bank would like you to believe, and in fact someone at the bank will probably try to tell you, that the lack of enthusiasm for small accounts fossilized in this table results from the increased cost of processing such trifles. Hmmm. On $1,000 the bank pays out $55.00 * (1/4) = $13.75 (this is a 90-day account); on $10,000 it pays out $215 and on $100,000 it pays out $2,800. Can you figure out the transaction cost to the bank, given that your

Table 1A Interest Rates for 90-day Certificates from One Bank in Mid-1983

Amount Invested	Interest Rate
Up to $1,000	5.5%
$1,000 to $2,500	7.5%
$2,500 to $25,000	8.6%
Over $25,000	11.2%

account is entered and paid on exactly once, by employees who were sitting around doing nothing when you walked in, on a computer the bank has to own or lease anyway? One way to look at it is that an ideal bank would pay you a proportional $28 on your $1,000—is the transaction cost then about $14? If so, why don't the $10,000 investors get more?

The real reason for this difference in rates is that people with more money have alternative investments to compare to bank deposits, and the bank thus has to compete harder for the big money. (What were you going to do with your measly $1,000, the bank sneers, buy a condo in Florida?)

The same problem will follow you if you try to take your money into the stock market on a plain transaction (to be honest, we will point out at once that you can do better than this at a discount brokerage firm or in a so-called no-load fund). Suppose you take a liking to a stock selling for about $15 per share, and have a mere $1,000 to do something about it. Your broker's commission at most places will be nearly 3% of the total, and since you won't be able to get a round lot (100 shares) you will pay an extra 12.5 cents per share on, let's say, 60 shares. The total commission will be $34.50. Because you will be paying this amount or perhaps a little more when you sell the stock, stock will have to go up more than a point for you to just break even. For a 10% yield on this investment the stock will have to make it to 17⅞, a price move of nearly 20%. The point here is that being able to pick stocks as well as that should entitle you to something a little better than standard bank interest, but the use of tiny sums militates against you.

If, on the other hand, you have $15,000 to use in the game, you will pay about $320 in commission for a thousand shares and about the same when you sell out. If the stock were to go to 17⅞ you would make a profit of $2,235, which is a clean 15%. (Please note: if you read nothing else in the rest of the book, observe that a discount broker would charge you about $100 each way and your yield would be closer to 18%.) This matter, which may seem to be an affair of only a few percentage points, is crucial because consistent performance a few percent better than average is all that is necessary—or perhaps even possible—to win what is essentially a struggle between you and all the other investors out there who are trying to do the same thing.

The examples of bank interest and brokerage fees are meant to explain why the figure $2,000 is the starting point for this chapter. There is such monumental and inescapable prejudice against small accounts at all types of financial institutions that your only hope of ever earning a return better than the inflation rate lies in somehow scraping together at least $2,000 or so. This exceedingly perishable reference, by the way, should become absolutely laughable as time goes on; $5,000 will be closer to the figure by 1990. But the point of requiring a minimum quantum of money to get a decent yield will probably always be relevant, and it will never be too difficult to determine the magic number.

A Few Words About Savings

At a randomly selected party, the subject of saving money is guaranteed to draw more certifiably lunatic conversation than any other subject, including religion, sex, politics, and sports. The reason for this bold assertion is that remarks are passed off with a tremendous air of conviction that are nonetheless quantifiable as nonsense. See if any of these examples sound familiar:

• A woman remarks that she just cannot abide paying $1.03 per roll for a particular type of paper towel when the same brand routinely sells for $0.91 at another store two miles away from the first one, so she makes a special trip to pick up a few rolls. Net travel expense in average car, $0.60; attempted savings on four rolls, $0.48. One hopes, additionally, that her time is exactly worthless, so as not to prejudice the accounting further.

- A gentleman with no other discernible trace of larceny in his heart routinely swipes from work a few ballpoint pens with the company name on them. These must be diligently concealed when higher-ups from the office are invited for dinner, as this is a company sore point. Average estimated savings per year, $3 to $5, depending on use; estimated aggravation and potential appearance of pettiness, anybody's guess.
- A family installs an $800 Norwegian woodstove and $350 worth of building-code-legal pipe for installation. They use three cords of wood at $120 per cord each winter for heating and thereby reduce their gas bill by $80 for each of five winter months (it develops, in this noble private experiment in physics, that the uninsulated hot-water pipes running under their house prevent their gas costs from going to zero as hoped). Net savings—somewhat equivocal. If the price of gas holds at the same level relative to the price of wood, this will all pay off in thirty years or so. If the price of wood starts to drift upward more rapidly, things are not quite so promising. Note: a) this is a real example from the across-the-street neighbors of one of the authors, and b) that's thirty years of cleaning out ashes every winter morning, on the way to the break-even point.

The point in these examples is, among other things, that the human heart takes disproportionate delight in tiny advantages. Ever have someone pass you on a road for the privilege of ending up ahead of you in line at a red light? Most examples of homely thrift, when boiled down to dollars per year, literally, won't buy you a pair of socks. Consider (this example is rather cruel, but it may have some pedagogical value) how much money you will save between the ages of twenty and seventy by extending the life of each tube of toothpaste you use by 5%. With the average current price of a medium-size tube around $1, you will save between 20 and 40 cents a year; multiply this by fifty for the lifetime total of $10 to $20, in current money. This magnificent sum, for a lifetime of standing in bathrooms cranking down those last few glops, thumbs tense and white!

The reason this is being brought up in this particularly embarrassing way is that it is practically impossible, for reasons probably as ancient as the first trade of mastodon meat for colored shells, to get some people to do any of the things that will actually save usable amounts of money. For example, if the prevailing mortgage rate is as much as one and one half points below the rate at which your mortgage was contracted, you would save, on the average American house in the mid-1980s, about $300 per year by refinancing. Yet all over this favored land, as sure as you are reading this, untold thousands will get up tomorrow morning, in houses with mortgages written at four points over the going rate (there are lots of them out there), and proceed to strangle the living daylights out of toothpaste tubes in a benighted attempt at economy.

A Few More Words on the Same Topic

A brief perusal of the tax tables will show you why saving is even more important than you think, difficult though it is to do. If you were to consult the tax tables for your 1984 return, you could note that a married couple filing jointly with $35,000 in taxable income was asked to pay $6,572 in taxes. The same couple, earning $36,000 instead, was supposed to pay $6,913. This means, quite explicitly, that in this region of the tax table, you have to come up with $1,000 to keep $659. Looked at in a closely related way, you have to earn $1.52 to have $1.00 to spend (or in most cases to save, under the remarkable tax laws of the good old U.S.A.).

Even in this tax bracket, which is by no means the absolute stratosphere, a penny saved is not a penny earned; it's about 1.5 cents. Everything you can do without or do more cheaply helps your finances by 50% more than the apparent savings. (If you consult the earlier work in this series, *Basic Money* [Seiter, Addison-Wesley, 1984], you could conclude that you save yourself about $220 in net income by walking away from a credit-card purchase of a $100 item, paid off at the minimum rate, when this tax effect is taken into account).

It is an old maxim in business that 10% of the effort produces 90% of the results, and the same is true of savings. Strangely enough, the same people who typically are willing to scrimp outrageously, saving old lunch bags and using month-old razor blades, apparently derive enough psychological satisfaction from these little physical manifestations of thrift that they don't worry about their backward savings strategies—all sorts of ten-cent savings are pursued and all sorts of major possibilities are overlooked.

Perhaps the most consistent way to approach this situation is to write out on a nice large sheet of paper the estimated cost *per year* of various supplies (this, by the way, is almost quintessentially a calculator-and-paper problem, although there are many computer packages available for it). Table 1B shows a sample of such a list.

Table 1B Sample List of Estimated Cost per Year of Various Supplies

Item	Highest Price	Lowest Price
Razor blades	$0.28	$0.17
	$14.56/yr.	$8.84/yr.
Dog food	$0.59/can	$0.42/can
	$431/yr.	$307/yr.
Gasoline	$1.41/gal.	$1.25/gal.
	$504/yr.	$446/yr.
Car insurance	$439/yr.	$321/yr.
Beer	Heineken	Budweiser
	$467/yr.	$342/yr.

The assumptions here are simple (you can change them to fit your own case). A razor blade is used for one week; the dog eats two cans per day; the car gets 28 miles per gallon and drives 10,000 miles per year; the car insurance numbers were simply the best and worst cases obtained in one afternoon from calling up six different companies in northern California. For the aggravation of worrying constantly about money you are rewarding yourself with two six-packs of beer per week, purchased in this example with no attempt at getting a particularly good price.

Please observe the conclusions. First, you can use any razor blades you want, and don't worry about getting one extra shave out of them. It just won't ever count. Second, you can probably find it convenient to buy dog food by the case anyway, and you will actually save reasonable amounts of money.

Third, it is always startling to observe the amount of effort that goes into gas mileage work as a source of savings—it certainly isn't worth running out of gas on your way to a cheaper gas station. Note also the difference in gas cost per year (a 10,000-mile year) between a car that averages 28 miles per gallon and one that gets 32 miles per gallon. It is something on the order of $50 per year at current (mid-1980s) gasoline prices. There is almost no known example of gasoline savings alone justifying the purchase of a new car; just the interest part of the typical financing deal on an average GM vehicle will be well over $1,000 per year. Trading in a 1964 Cadillac hearse for the most fuel-efficient Honda may have aesthetic benefits but won't actually balance out on mileage considerations alone, remarkably enough.

Note also that if you take the initiative to get your car insurance changed to the cheapest form you may get to treat yourself to Heineken for a year (no judgment of beer quality implied by that statement). This example is specifically important because it calls up the fact that paperwork savings are frequently the most painless to obtain in daily life. Would it impact your daily life in any unpleasant way if somehow your housing payments were reduced by $30 per month? This is a real possibility for a great many people. As you make out your chart of possible savings per year, do you see anything that promises to deliver savings of that magnitude?. One of the defining premises of the earlier book, *Basic Money*, was that reduction of finance costs is the easiest way to produce meaningful savings—it still is true, and this book will extend the concept to insurance and other forms of "paperwork payments" that form a surprisingly large part of household budgets. It's amazing how little can be saved, for example, by skimping on food, compared to the potential savings in a close inspection of financial instruments.

In any case, to evaluate whether some procedure for savings is worthwhile, it is pretty much a necessity to run up estimates of possible savings over a whole year rather than focusing on single-purchase savings. This approach will also appear in other sections of this book; in tax situations, for example, we will emphasize looking at the amount of money you finally get to keep by different strategies, rather than looking at tax reduction only from different maneuvers. There is an important difference.

What to Do with $2,000 in Savings

We will run through seven different possible actions and then summarize them briefly. These seven possibilities will represent, roughly, the kinds of opportunities that present themselves at moderate savings levels. To a certain extent, your reaction to these situations amounts to a sort of personality inventory: do you find yourself comforted or bored by the idea of small but steady gains? . . . Do you find yourself thrilled or horrified by the prospect of a roller coaster ride in the commodities market?

The topics for consideration are: simple savings, IRA savings, stock purchase, IRA stock, corn futures, gold, and house payments.

FIRST CASE
Simple Savings

We will suppose for the purpose of having a standard test case that you are married, filing a joint return, on a taxable income of $35,000 per year. Under no circumstances should you consider getting married solely to match this condition for ease of reference, nor should you turn down a higher paying job to fit this profile; it has been selected because it matches the readership profile of a middle-of-the-road computer magazine. Not only will there be suggestions in this chapter on how to adjust the results to your own case, but in fact the whole rest of the book will consist of programs for sharpening up these computations.

If you have saved $2,000 under these typical circumstances, the first thing you must do is consider that you will be paying taxes on it. You can figure the taxes first and set them aside or invest the whole $2,000 and turn your investment back into cash before April 15. Since this second way is the simplest, that's what we will do. We will also assume that you will find an 8.5% time deposit. Interest rates will float many points up and down during what is hoped will be the useful life of this book, but we will mainly be concerned with comparisons of the relative prospects of different investments, so the qualitative results will still be correct, even if the rate goes to 7.2%, 13%, or something more extreme.

In any event, at the rate stated above, you have $2,170

at the end of the year (the rate 8.5% was an *effective annual yield*—just check a newspaper ad for a savings and loan and you will invariably see this number and a slightly smaller one called the *annual rate*. This will all be explained later). Now the question is simply how much of this you should consider to be due for taxes. The bank will forward a little note to the IRS saying that you have made $170, and you thus are presumably paying taxes on this amount. But the fact is that the original $2,000 was income that you earned in the first place, and it appears on an earnings statement, for example, a W–2, from some other source.

To further complicate this question (the real advice at this point is to leave it all in the bank, if you can) there is the problem that, although the tax rate at $35,000 is 18.8%, for a tax of $6,572 the so-called marginal rate is about 33%. The marginal rate, referred to indirectly in the section above on savings, is the rate at which your money is disappearing to the government off the top: each dollar beyond the $35,000 is taxed at about a 33% rate, and this increase is how, eventually, you end up in the maximum bracket. An understanding of this may or may not truly be necessary in evaluating your options. The marginal rate is a useful concept in economics, but now that it is possible to evaluate your total taxes on your total income very quickly by using a computer, familiarity with this concept may not be as necessary in personal finance as it once was.

Anyway, the results are that, considered as straight tax, the government will take about $407 from the $2,170 in your account, and considered at the marginal rate the tax is about $645. Remember, the taxes have to come from somewhere, whether you leave the money in the account or not. Once you have some money to invest, you have to consider the composition of your sources of income and their contribution to your tax burden. Taking the most optimistic view, by saving $2,000 at interest you at least have $1,763 to show for yourself after taxes instead of the $1,624 you would have had if you had kept the money in an old sock under your bed. Of course, this doesn't take into account the depreciation in the value of the money due to inflation, but in an odd way this doesn't count, because neither you nor your economic competitors can do anything about it. This will be the basic case for comparison, and in fancier versions later on we will begin thinking about inflation.

SECOND CASE
IRA Savings

This one is fairly simple, because there are by definition no tax considerations to ponder. Everything here, needless to say, applies also to Keogh accounts (which are in several ways more flexible and interesting than IRAs). You put your $2,000 in an individual retirement account. The first effect of this is to reduce your tax bill for the year by $600 (that's the difference between the tax on $35,000 and the tax on $33,000). In a truly hard-core version of the computation, we would insist that you now put $2,500 instead of $2,000 in the account in celebration of the good news, but perhaps you would rather do something fun and exciting such as roof repair or making insurance payments, so that $2,000 is still the figure.

On the $2,000 you can probably find an account that pays 11% (if the regular accounts are paying 8.5%), so at the end of the year you will have $2,220. This is certainly a tremendous improvement on the amount you had in the earlier case. There are just two catches: a) you don't know what the tax rate will be on this money when you try to get it out when you retire (how much per month will you need to get after age 59½?), and b) if you want the money now, there are a variety of penalties, some from the bank and some from the federal government. In a typical penalty scheme, if you have left the money in for one year and a day, the bank will pay you no interest at all for the first six months and 5¼ percent on the other six months; this gives you $2,052 or so as you walk out the door. But the IRS now wants a penalty payment of 10% of this, say $205 for simplicity, and you will pay taxes on the withdrawn balance as regular income. The correct amount to consider that you are paying in taxes now is exactly the amount you considered that you had saved before by starting the IRA account, namely $600. The total that you get to keep if you need the money after one year is therefore $2,052 − $205 − $600 = $1,247.

So there are strong disincentives for taking your money out of an IRA before retirement (this is called a premature distribution). First, the bank will just about cancel (probably with considerable glee) all the interest you would have earned, and second, the IRS 10% penalty on top of your normal tax rate makes this the most highly-taxed money you could have this year. If we play strictly fair and consider the money in the regular (non-IRA) account above as being taxed at the marginal rate, you really only have $2,170 − $645 = $1,525 dollars in that account anyway, but even so, the difference as a percent of your total is discouragingly large. Everyone, from the financial institutions to the government, wants you to keep that money in the retirement account.

THIRD CASE
Stock Purchase

Let us suppose that for six months you have conscientiously read all relevant material about a particular industrial domain, say electronics, and have closely examined the business prospects of a selected group of companies in the industry. Now you feel ready to make a few stock selections. Or, conversely, perhaps you have never studied any of these things in your life, but your barber tells you that his brother-in-law says that Allied Datatronics, Intergalactic Semiconductor, and Zyzplex are about to take off big. Now you feel ready to make a few stock selections.

You take your $2,000 to a brokerage office and plunk it down on Zyzplex, selling at $18 per share. A one-hundred-share lot will carry a commission of about $50 at a middle-of-the-road firm (not a discount house but not one of the most expensive ones). Zyzplex executes a random walk over the space of a year and ends up at $22 per share, a gain of slightly more than 20%. Let us suppose, however, that you have executed this maneuver in one of two possible ways. In Scenario 1, you got very edgy after the stock started dropping three months after you bought it, so you sold it at $13 and then got back on board a few weeks later when it began climbing past $15. In this scheme you thus have two transactions. In Scenario 2 you have nerves of steel, eyes of flint, gravel in your guts, and the personality of a hibernating granite block, so you ride out the stock to a year and a day before selling.

The concern here over the length of time the stock is held has to do with taxes. If you hold the stock for more than six months (1984 rules) you are, in the eyes of the IRS, an "investor," a responsible and socially desirable citizen who deserves a break on his or her taxes; only 40% of so-called long-term capital gains are taxable. On the other hand, if you are the type of flighty individual who trades in and out every few months, you are a "speculator," and the money you make, if any, is going to be taxed at the same regular-income rates as you pay on the tips you get playing piano in the cathouse down the road.

Let's compare the two scenarios.

Scenario 1:
Loss on first trade = $500 ((18 − 13) * 100 shares)
Commissions = $100
Profit on second trade = $700 ((22 − 15) * 100 shares)
Commissions = $100

The commissions appear in this way because you get nicked for $50 on both buying and selling the stock. Your position in this case is that you have earned $200 in short-term capital gains, which will be taxed as ordinary income (not to mention, of course, that the original $2,000 you used to start this business will itself also be taxable). Using the marginal rate (which means, again, comparing your taxes at $35,200 to your taxes at $33,000) we find that the government gets $645 of the whole package. Including the $200 in brokerage commissions, which is unfortunately non-deductible, Scenario 1 leaves you with $1,355 from the before-taxes $2,000. The real point in this exercise is that trading frequently has eaten up your modest profit.

To ram this point home, consider the second possibility.

Scenario 2:
Profit on trade = $400 ((22 − 18) * 100 shares)
Commissions = $100

This profit, taken in a stock you held for more than six months, is long-term; thus you get to keep 60% of it. Your position is that you have to pay tax on the original $2,000 and on 40% of the profits, or $160. The tables report the by-now-notorious figure of $645 again as taxes, so your net position for this investment adventure (the "romance of capitalism," as a brochure once proclaimed) is $2,400 − $645 (tax) − $100 (commissions) = $1,655. That's not so bad, considering that: a) if you had just kept the money in a peanut-butter jar you would have paid $600 in taxes and been left with only $1,400, and b) you are $300 ahead of the two-trade case, basically with the same judgment on the same stock. Even so, it is clearly seen in these two examples that being a pipsqueak in the market is tough; the commissions in and out amount to a 5% barrier you have to overcome just to break even.

Stock Market IRA

We can compare the results of these two scenarios when the investments are taking place in an IRA account rather than a standard brokerage account. There is no particular problem doing this; brokerage firms have been falling all over themselves in their haste to come up with miraculously flexible and convenient "vehicles" for investment. Many of these accounts do have desirable features (for example, they may put the balance not in stocks into a money-market account while you wait for your next inspiration), but these will be discussed in a later chapter.

When the stocks are traded in an IRA account the effect is that they are put beyond the reach of taxes. In Scenario 1 you would end up with exactly $2,000 in your account at the end of your peregrinations, because you made a $200 profit on the transactions and paid $200 in commissions. In Scenario 2 you would have your $400 profit minus $100 in brokerage fees, leaving $2,300 at the end of the year.

Two curious points arise in connection with the stock market IRA. First, notice that it really no longer makes any difference whether your gains are short term or long term, because you are not paying taxes on any of this any more. This can make your experiences in the market more congenial; one of the most agonizing experiences available is watching a successful stock start to dribble downward as you try to hang on to it for the long term. In an IRA you can get out whenever you want with no tax penalties.

Second, although the legal situation may someday be changed by persistent lobbying by banking organizations, it is easier to get your money out in the despised "premature distribution." When you want your money back from the usual savings IRA, the bank will haul off most of the interest you have earned; the amount varies from one bank to the next but is usually sufficiently gruesome as to discourage such action. In a stock IRA the brokerage house doesn't try to take your stock profits (although in some cases there are special fees). All you have to do in this case is face the IRS penalty of 10% on the amount withdrawn and then pay the usual income taxes on that amount. The IRS penalty and the implicit internal cost of brokerage commissions are certainly a disincentive to withdrawing early on the spur of the moment, but at least you get clobbered only about half as badly in this case as you do at a bank or savings and loan.

FIFTH CASE
Corn Futures

What follows could not be recommended as a truly prudent course of action, and in fact under current conditions it is probably not even something you can try (the entrance fee for this game has recently been raised), but it is, we hope, instructive material that has at least as much to do with the reality of the investment world as do certificates of deposit and grandmotherly mutual funds.

Here are the mechanics of a corn futures deal, as practiced at a middle-of-the-road brokerage house in the mid-1980s (this business has changed considerably over the last decade or so, as efforts to protect the lambs from the wolves or from their own erring lamb-like judgment have been implemented). For $2,500 you can get two corn futures contracts, because the standard corn contract at the moment is $1,250. For the sake of argument, we will take March corn at $3.10. You buy these contracts in December, so you have about three months to watch the price of corn for March delivery (you will never get any corn—you are essentially obliged to clear out before the delivery date). Every day you can consult the newspapers and check the price of a March corn contract as it goes up or down, typically by a few cents.

What you have purchased is the amount that the price fluctuates on a standard corn contract, which is 5,000 bushels. When the price of corn goes, up by one cent, you have made $50, that is, $0.01 * 5,000, on each of your two contracts. Can you guess what happens when the price goes down by one cent? That's right. And if the price goes down by a quarter, you have just lost the amount you put down on each contract in your account at the brokerage firm, as $0.25 * 5000 = $1,250. They will call you up and ask if you want to put more money in the account and keep on playing, or whether you want to close out at zero, sadder but wiser.

Please note carefully what has happened in the melancholic example of the above-mentioned two-bit price drop. The price of March corn has gone, hypothetically, from $3.10 to $2.85, a drop of 8% or so. Your account, on the other hand, is completely wiped out. That is because it is a so-called margin account, in which you put up only a small fraction of the value of the commodity in question. The whole price of the real corn contract at 5,000 bushels is more like $15,000; that's the amount of money that will deliver something to feed the hogs. What you have done is to put up about 8% of the total price, and you get the full value of the price changes on the total contract—that's why you can be wiped out on an 8% drop.

Of course, if March corn goes from $3.10 to $3.35 (a price rise of a mere twenty-five cents once more) you have *doubled* your money in a few short months, something that is nearly impossible to do in the stock market and by definition impossible in a bank investment. In practice, about 80% of commodities speculators end up losing money. For this reason, you will probably find that the brokerage house will want you to leave $10,000 or so in a cash account with them while you find out how good you are at this sort of thing.

The reasons you are not likely to do very well at this are interesting, one structural and one purely mathematical. The structural reason is that there are two parties on each end of a transaction, and in the commodities market in grain, for example, the other end of your contract is likely to be a huge grain-trading conglomerate that gets field reports and midwestern weather news every fifteen minutes. You may beat these guys, but you won't beat them by much and you won't beat them often. An analogous but somewhat less severe problem exists in the stock market, in which some stock moves are determined by insider trades of dubious legality. In corn futures, the real insider is the farmer, and he can trade all he wants with no discouragement from the Feds.

The mathematical problem is that the size of the price movement per day is large enough that you could be wiped out even if your initial judgment is correct. You may buy the corn contract in December at $3.10 expecting it to go to $3.50 before you sell out (at a nice profit). The problem is that if the price goes through $2.80 or so first, you will be at zero, and it would take an almost unreasonable confidence in your judgment to toss more money into the hopper at this point and hang on until you were proved correct.

If, on the other hand, you bought a stock at $31 per share, it is unlikely that you would be scared out by a drop to $28 as you waited for an eventual rise to $35. You wouldn't make anywhere near as much money, but you wouldn't be cleaned out unless the company actually died. Continuing the argument, you could have put the money in a time deposit and have a guaranteed small profit and no possibility of loss.

Thus there exists a hierarchy of uses for your money, with high-risk/high-reward situations at one extreme and low-risk/low-reward situations at the other. This is an ongoing theme in this book, and we will attempt to pick out situations in which there are clear advantages, either in minimizing risk or maximizing return. It's not always easy, but that's what you have to do. As a parting piece of advice, pick out three commodities contracts for yourself and follow them on paper for a few months or so. Unless you are ridiculously lucky or outrageously astute, you should emerge from the game absolutely fascinated by mutual funds and insurance stocks.

SIXTH CASE
Gold

It is an enlightening experience to keep old financial newspapers and magazines. A perusal of the last few years' worth of journals would yield many breathless articles about the prospects of microcomputer companies that are no longer with us; predictions about coming booms, recessions, and wild fluctuations in the interest rate; and evidence of the unquenchable fascination with precious metals. As this is written, against the background of a gold price of around $400, the computer used for programming rests on a desk next to twenty-three articles predicting gold prices from $600 to $2,500 per ounce, for this time. It is worth keeping in mind that the articles you read today are the old articles of next year.

Yet people have lots of faith in gold, and in the mid-1980s it is hard for many people to forget the spectacular rise in gold prices a few years ago. That rise could have been a one-time speculative binge, linked to the massive dislocations in international cash flow that accompanied the oil price increases of the late 1970s. It is also possible that the thorough determination of industry to use as little gold as possible when the price goes up will act forever as a brake on gold prices (the computer you use to try out the programs in this book probably contains some gold as circuit-card contacts—and you should know that the company that made the board has a gold substitute all lined up in case of a jump in the price of gold). Although technically gold is just another commodity, like the corn that made the basis of the futures contract above, it is at least something you can actually hold; $2,000 worth of gold coins won't even make an appreciable lump in your coat pocket.

With $2,000 you could buy four to six Krugerrands, depending on market condition, or about the same number of the nearly equivalent Austrian coronas. In an absolutely hilarious piece of protect-the-rich legislation, coin purchases over $1,000 pay no sales tax in many states (California is a good example). All you would have to consider under these circumstances as an impediment to your potential profits is the difference between buy and sell prices, typically $15 to $20. This means that you buy a coin for $400, and if you wanted to sell it ten minutes later to the same dealer he would pay you $380 for it (it represents an implicit service charge).

Given that $2,000 should let you earn bank interest about five points higher than the inflation rate under many circumstances, an inflation rate of 6% would get you 11% for $220 in interest profit on a deposit. A similar amount, say five gold coins at $400 each, will return this amount if the price of gold goes up about 16% (that's because you need $100 to cover the buy/sell spread on the coins—16% would give you $320, but you lose this amount up front).

This example, although of course the exact numbers change all the time, points out a possible problem; it calls for an inflation rate for gold that is three times the rate for other goods in general. And that's just to *match* the bank rate. Because you are risking your money on this (gold does go down, too) you undoubtedly are looking for more profit than you could get in a bank in an insured account. On the other hand, if the economy is more or less collapsing and the inflation rate is out of control, gold may look like a really astute move. Just keep in mind that if everything stays glued together, and the Soviet Union and South Africa still need to generate foreign exchange by selling gold, the price could just rise and fall unspectacularly, on a time scale of years and years and years. Furthermore, if gold prices just follow the approximate inflation rate, you can then trade them in only for dollars, which are worth proportionately less—no real gain. This is the economic end of the ethical argument on investment; in principle you *shouldn't* be guaranteed of making real money for hoarding metal, and there are reasons to expect that in general there are more productive uses for your funds.

SEVENTH CASE
Real Estate

There is an interesting maneuver that should not be dismissed immediately, although at first glance it appears to be absolute lunacy. This consists of looking at your home mortgage, taking a deep breath, and sending $2,000 to your loan officer with the instruction that it is to be applied to the principal on your home loan (assuming you have one).

Why, you might ask, in the sacred name of Citibank, would you want to do a thing like that? The argument depends on a combination of things, of which the principal elements are your mortgage interest rate, how long you have held the mortgage, and the rate your local bank is currently paying on deposits. Let us suppose that you are sitting on a $60,000 mortgage financed at 16%. (That's a little high, but there are plenty of them out there, and there will be in the future, too.) Over thirty years, the total of payments will be $290,000 or so. If you send the bank $2,000 and apply it to the principal near the beginning of the loan, say the first six years, this $2,000 will save you a total of $9,666 in payments over the life of the loan. If the best you could get on a $2,000 deposit would be 7% or so, the advantages of this are pretty clear.

To recapitulate: if you have a home mortgage, it means you owe a large sum of money to a bank or savings and loan. The bank is charging you interest on this sum. If the mortgage is fairly recent (we are not talking about the last year of a 6% dreamboat mortgage left over from the 1960s), you are certainly paying interest at a higher rate than the bank would be willing to pay you on a deposit. That is almost the complete definition of what the bank is supposed to do. The idea of taking in money on an IRA you can't touch for twenty years, paying 9% on it, and lending it back to you in a 14% home loan, is one that is enough to give a grown man in a pin-striped three-piece suit an involuntary fit of the giggles.

So, you get the picture? If you have bought a home recently, *you* are one of the best investments around. In fact you can't by definition find anything that will pay you as much as the bank is earning from you. Few people are aware that they can make payments of this kind without invoking fees or refinance charges, but a survey of ten major banks in various states will show you that the loan officers know all about this sort of thing and are not especially surprised at this kind of question. The trick here is to figure out how to decide if this is worth doing when the rates are fairly close. A scheme for doing this will appear in the chapter later in this book on real estate, but in the meanwhile you may regard it as something to spark your curiosity.

2
The Nature of Investment

There are a number of philosophical issues in investment, and we will now spend a few minutes to consider them before plunging into the realm of straightforward calculations about money. The reason for doing this is that, although this book is called *Advanced Money,* it will be recognized by even the most hard-boiled readers that money itself is only a means to nonmonetary satisfactions, and questions of the "Larger Issues of Life" are always lurking in the background, even of works whose aims are as modest as those unfolded here.

Introductory Sermonette

Suppose that a firm has $80,000 at its disposal and is thinking of alternative uses for it, here starkly considered as a choice between two purchases: it can buy $80,000 worth of gold and sit on it for a year, or it can buy an automated milling machine for $75,000 and a training course from the manufacturer for $5,000. Now it must be noted immediately that although the gold is an investment, meaning that a year later it may be sold for more than its purchase price, it is really quite an antisocial use of money. The firm becomes no more productive, and the increase in nominal value of the gold is probably just an index of inflation. "Investments" of this nonproductive kind have in fact become quite popular with firms that have lots of cash; when oil companies found themselves awash in money a few years ago they began buying up apartment buildings in areas already plagued with severe real-estate inflation. A more recent oil-company approach is to buy smaller oil companies. Neither of these activities appears to have generated much benefit for the companies, and it would be a cheerful fellow indeed who could claim to see much benefit for the public.

An investment in new equipment, if properly planned, can on the other hand be of great benefit to everyone. The milling machine and training can allow the development of a more efficient way to produce needed products and at the same time make employees more productive and their work more pleasant. Furthermore, if the firm knows what it is doing it should be able to make more money designing and manufacturing products than sitting on a gold hoard.

The Past Becomes the Future

It is time to review for a moment an example of investment behavior that has been rendered picturesque by the passage of time. The dynamics of this tale will be identical to those of recent new stock issues in computers and in genetic engineering, and doubtless, if we had better historical sources, could be compared to Carthaginian adventures in the trade in purple murex dye.

Most of what follows may be studied at greater length in the book *Extraordinary Popular Delusions and the Madness of Crowds,* a work issued in London in 1841 by an exceptionally perceptive gentleman named Charles Mackay. Because Mackay's work is the most readable account of the speculative binges of the dawn of capitalism, it attained a certain gloomy notoriety in investing circles following the stock market crash of 1929. It is difficult to believe that it will be any less relevant two hundred years from now, if we're still here. Any reputable investment book should direct the reader to this lively antique as a first course.

We will consider the career of the amazing John Law, a Scottish gambler and economic theorist who at one time was essentially entrusted with the entire French economy. Born in 1671, Law succeeded in gambling away his family's estate by his early twenties. But he was undeniably brilliant; he issued at one point a tract proposing the creation of a Land Bank in Scotland, that is, a bank that would issue paper money that was backed by deeds of trust to an equivalent value in land. The plan was not adopted, and Law's unsuccessful gambling, successful duelling, and apparently tremendous levels of appreciation by other people's wives all combined to make an extended stay on the Continent appear attractive. There he practiced gambling in the major European centers until he came to be regarded as one of the most skillful gamblers in Europe.

In the course of a stay in Paris, Law became a card-playing friend of many French noblemen. One of these noblemen was the Duke of Orléans, who upon the death of Louis XIV became Regent of France. He found the treasury hopelessly in debt and the revenues of the government pathetically insufficient for servicing even the interest part of the national debt. (Is this story at all familiar? Any heavy parallels to be drawn?) The Duke tried, therefore, a few experiments in currency devaluation and an inquiry into the amount that French tax collectors were keeping back for themselves. These efforts had the effect of bringing internal economic activity to a standstill and spreading an incredible amount of ill will and suspicion.

The time was definitely ripe for Law's notions of banking to be given a test. In 1716 Law & Company was given the right to issue paper money; Law himself attempted to make sure not only that the money was backed by real value but that the notes would always be redeemable for what they were worth at the time of issuance, that is, they couldn't be devalued. This approach, which is of course something like the definitional essence of honest banking, was an instant success, and Law's bank soon had branches all over France. The availability of guaranteed paper money induced commercial confidence and a great revival of trade ensued.

Unfortunately, the popularity of this enterprise induced the Duke, as Regent, to reformulate the whole package as the Royal Bank of France, in which he had at least as much authority as Law. And one of the Duke's first gestures with the new bank was to issue exactly twenty times as much paper money as was prudent in Law's estimate. This piece of mischief by itself would have been enough to destabilize things pretty severely, but the plot really gets interesting at this point.

France had just embarked on some global explorations, establishing trading stations in India and the Far East; of course, the country also had a large stake in Canada and the Louisiana Territory. Thus, the state authorized the formation of the Mississippi Company, originally in reference to Louisiana but later applying to all France's overseas enterprises, which was to be a stock company in which people could buy shares to participate in the vast profits from colonial commerce. In particular, it was hoped perhaps that some of the recently printed "funny money" could be reabsorbed through purchase of Mississippi shares, and, for that matter, backed in the bank by some of the huge supply of gold that was imagined to lie just outside of New Orleans. (The wealth of the Natchez Indians raised false hopes in early French explorers.)

Absolutely everyone who heard of the Mississippi Company wanted shares, and their value began to climb. Because buying these certain-to-rise, sure-thing shares was an automatic way of making money, the demand became furious. The street in front of the issuing office was thronged day and night; noblemen waited patiently (or impatiently) in their carriages for an audience with Law, and even poor tradesmen waited to invest their life savings in a few shares. The only subject of gossip in Paris, a town that usually has plenty of other things to gossip about, was the fabulous fountain of wealth and its overnight production of millionaires. The office had to move to more spacious and remote quarters.

What follows is sufficiently classic that it probably should be printed on plastic card stock for ready perpetual reference. First, many of the leading noblemen of France, having plenty of reason to doubt the sagacity of the government of which they were a part, began quietly unloading Mississippi and India Company shares; numerous magnificent chateaux on the Loire owe their splendor to profits of the year 1719. Second, the government found that it had to keep printing more paper money in order to support the constant rise in share prices; thus, a large fraction of all the money in the country was involved in the purchase of shares. Third, one prominent figure became angry over problems in buying more shares and in disgust sold his current shares and then demanded payment in coin for his paper money. This immediately threatened to raise the troublesome issue that by this point there could not have been enough silver on the planet to back the ocean of currency sloshing around France.

Although this first incident was managed somehow, by early 1720 many people were deciding in the interests of prudence to cash in shares and currency and stash the coins and other precious metal in foreign countries. To stop this practice, the authorities produced a remarkable law that limited the amount of coinage that could be owned by individuals. At this point it dawned even on the dimmest that something might be wrong. A trickle of stock-share sell-outs became a flood, and the price of Mississippi shares collapsed, bankrupting the great numbers of people who couldn't get out fast enough.

The government finally produced a plan to trade Mississippi shares at a great discount for bonds on the revenues of the city of Paris, a development that was accepted with much grumbling as at least better than nothing. Law himself was compelled for reasons of safety to leave France; he appears actually to have been reasonably honest throughout the whole enterprise and was not in fact one of those who cashed in early. He died penniless in Venice in 1729. There are people issuing stock in new companies today compared to whom Law was a saint and a wise man.

We will see shortly that it was no accident that the rise and fall of the remarkable Mississippi Company followed this particular course. Virtually at the same time, a similar tale by the name of the "South Sea Bubble" (*bubble* because of its explosive demise) was occupying the attention of the presumably more phlegmatic population of England. The time-averaged course of red-hot speculations can be modeled on a few fairly unimpeachable assumptions about human nature, and the consequences of these assumptions are so powerful as to thwart any intervention, government or otherwise.

The example of John Law has a certain charm, coming as it does from the dawn of paper-money capitalism. It will not do, please note, to conclude that people in the eighteenth century were somehow excitable or naive. "Sure-thing, can't-miss" investments are, if anything, more available now than they were centuries ago. In early 1984, in a sort of primitive tribute to the power of these economic events, a curious news article came over the wire-service lines. Apparently two men kidnapped their stock broker—a fellow who had succeeded in losing them hundreds of thousands of dollars over the years with fabulous tips on dynamic stocks—and kept him for nearly two weeks in a basement torture chamber before abandoning him. Who can say what particular sins brought on this fate?

A meticulously documented version of a scam with less intrinsic good intent than the Mississippi affair was the attempt within the last decade to corner the silver market, an adventure that at least had the redeeming feature of causing a good deal of economic pain to its organizers. And, reader, you may well believe that the future will furnish more examples, necessitating the treatment in the section about to follow.

What Goes Up . . .

An interesting feature of the French farce described above (actually there was nothing funny about it, to the participants, anyway) is that the price sequence in time of the Mississippi shares followed the exact course typical of all booms. This is worth examining in detail, since the phenomenon occurs in classic form every few years or so. Florida real estate in the 1920s, stocks such as Comsat in the go-go stock market of the late 1960s, silver in the late 1970s, and some red-hot, sure-fire thing this year are all stock examples of the working-out of a fairly simple set of rules that govern speculation.

We will describe in some detail how this works, but we'll omit the actual BASIC program (available for your inspection in the earlier work, *Basic Money*). As it happens, it's fairly easy to see, qualitatively, how the forces of crowd psychology drive the price of some speculation. Here are the factors to take into account:

Greed As soon as some "investment" (we will call this one Wonderstock) becomes widely recognized as one that is bound to go up, there will be a demand for it. The formation stage of this situation is often murky, but once it happens it is unmistakable. There are articles in newspapers and business magazines talking about Wonderstock, describing the way "smart money" is moving into it. This typically means that managers of growth-oriented mutual funds, for example, are buying Wonderstock. As the price goes up, needless to say, more people become convinced that the price will go up, and this increased demand for Wonderstock makes the price go up further.

Limitation The demand for Wonderstock causes the price to rise at a certain rate. With every price increase, however, the prospect arises that some people will simply not be able to scratch up enough money to get in on this fabulous deal. Although the market in Wonderstock may expand rapidly for some time, the finite number of swingers in the universe and the finite amount of money available to them means that at some point the effective demand for Wonderstock slows down. When the rate of price increase slows, this speculation has hit a dangerous point. That is, the price may still be going up, but it is going up more slowly or more irregularly.

Fear So the price has gone up, but the rate of increase is no longer as spectacular as it once was. At this point, speculators who got in on Wonderstock at the beginning are looking at a nice potential profit if they get out now; the fund managers who picked out this little gem can unload it and look absolutely brilliant. Some quiet and modulated unloading of the stock begins. Please note that by the "iron law of the market" there is some hopeful character buying every share that someone is selling. Somewhere out there are people who have bought any given stock at its historic peak. Anyway, in the career of every Wonderstock there comes a delicate moment at which it is quietly being sold by people who know that a good thing won't last forever. This slows the price rise, makes many people nervous, more stock begins to sell, and the price starts going down. The drop in price panics more speculators, who begin dumping Wonderstock in an attempt not to get stuck with a loss, and the market in Wonderstock becomes "disorderly." In the well-regulated modern world, trading in Wonderstock may be suspended altogether so that it doesn't set a bad example for the other securities or damage "investor confidence."

The astute or cynical reader will at once note a certain formal resemblance of this kind of speculative binge to the venerable "chain letter" or its close relative, the pyramid scheme. In a chain-letter plan, you get a letter asking you to send money to some names on a letter, and then a longer list of people will get a letter from you and supposedly send you some money. In fact people who are at the beginning of a chain will collect a lot of money before the chain dies out. And it *must* die out at some point because the number of potential letter recipients is limited, at least by the population of the earth. The largest single group of participants in a chain letter will be those in the last round, the group that sends out much more money than it ever takes in. The Wonderstock example and its analogues identify as the largest single group of "investors" those who have bought the stock at or near its peak price. That, dear reader, is a real lesson to chew on—if you can convince yourself of the similarities between wildly popular investments and chain letters this book will have been your best investment in years.

By the way, there is a simple method for determining the point at which Wonderstock crosses the line from investment to speculation. The stock reports in many newspapers, and in the *Wall Street Journal* in particular, list the price/earnings ratio for the stock as well as the price. If this number is somewhere between, say, seven and fifteen, it means that Wonderstock corporation is out there selling products and earning money on them, at a rate that is at least better than would be obtained by selling off all the assets and sticking them in a bank.

If this ratio, on the other hand, is one hundred or so, and the stock is still climbing steadily, then Wonderstock is a crapshoot pure and simple—no one is expecting to get back his money from this economic miracle by waiting around to collect dividends (because these will be tiny or nonexistent). If there are no earnings, as in the case of consistent losses, or no products, as in the case of many new high-tech issues, then rapid price movement may be taken as a fairly sure sign that the ghost of the Mississippi Company is hovering over the market.

A Quasi-mathematical Summary

The principles of greed, limitation, and fear can be summarized in a rather pitiless expression for the price of a commodity (or stock, or antique vase, or whatever). The expression

PRICENOW = PRICEBEFORE * OPTIMISM * LIMITATION

may be explained as follows. We pick a starting price as PRICEBEFORE, say $1 for simplicity. In the next price round this will be multiplied by the factors OPTIMISM and LIMITATION. OPTIMISM is a number that accounts for the belief that prices are rising; it is greater than one (driving up PRICENOW) as long as PRICENOW is greater than PRICEBEFORE for the previous round. The possibility of PRICENOW starting to drop is contained in the term LIMITATION. LIMITATION also contains the term PRICENOW and begins to drop as PRICENOW grows rapidly, reflecting the fact that at high enough prices more and more people are simply squeezed out

Figure 2A Price History of a Volatile Market

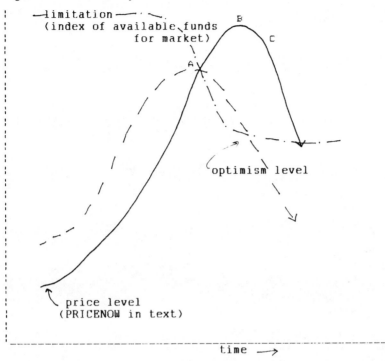

of the pool of potential speculators. When LIMITATION be-comes noticeably less than one, PRICENOW starts dropping, which in turn makes OPTIMISM drop even faster, and finally this simple model crashes (the price starts to go negative). Actually, although negative prices are not realistic, the notion of a total crash at the end of a speculative binge is quite appropriate. In the stock market crash of 1929, it was impossible to establish any price at all for most stocks while the collapse was going on; there were simply no buyers to be found, even for major "blue-chip" stocks.

Figures 2A and 2B illustrate this price career for two examples, one tuned for a really volatile market and one for a somewhat statelier progression. Figure 2A shows not only the price but also the relative scale for OPTIMISM and LIMITATION. An incredible amount of gossip, news, and speculation always accompanies a phenomenon like this, which is in fact simply the mechanical working-out of a few simple principles. Note particularly that the optimism level rolls over several steps before the price starts to fall (point a). This reflects accurately the perception of experienced market players that a slowdown

Figure 2B Price History for a Modest Boom

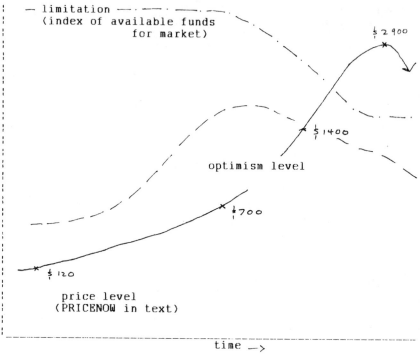

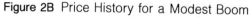

in the rate of increase means the beginning of the "delicate" period in the history of this issue (point b). The people who understand what is happening begin unloading their stake in the investment at this point, but the price keeps rising as others, whom we will charitably think of as "poorly informed," crowd in for the last few moments of financial glory. There are always, in well-publicized cases of this type, plenty of articles in newspapers and financial journals at the beginning of the slide (point c), reassuring nervous investors that this situation will only be a "hiccup" and that things will soon be right. In the crash of 1929 an impressive array of government officials, economists, and bankers trotted before the general public to calm its fears. There are probably mathematical rules of noneconomic behavior that demand this, if we only knew more about ourselves.

Figure 2B shows a version of the same phenomenon that is distinguished from the previous case only by a much slower start. The point in displaying this is to show, among other things, how much easier it is, requiring much less judgment and not-necessarily-hyperacute market timing, to make money by being in at the beginning rather than at the volatile middle.

If you bought into this little deal near $120 or so and closed out at $700, well before the peak, you would have taken your stake up by nearly a factor of seven. If you bought in at $1,400, the point at which it would be the recognized hot topic of the year, and sold out in a miracle of perspicacity right near the peak (around $2,900) you would have only doubled your money despite taking truly heart-stopping risks. As a general principle, this is why it is so easy to get burned repeatedly in the stock market on just those stocks which are considered the best speculative bets.

The Mathematics of Less Interesting Cases

A model in which the price of an investment (here, for the sake of argument, considered to be a stock) surges upward and then crashes dramatically is, however, appropriate to only a handful of cases per year. What the run-of-the-mill stock is doing in an average year is quite different, but the behavior of average stocks is a matter of controversy. One school of thought contends that the movement of a stock's price is totally random, jumping up or down over periods of time in a way that cannot be predicted in principle. The other school contends that the price histories of stocks contain interesting recognizable features; these features are rather like those shown in Figures 2A and 2B.

Actually, a point that perhaps overrides the considerations of mathematical psychology on which a correct resolution of this would depend is the question "What good will this do anyway?" If stock prices have a largely random character, this at least simplifies your selection method, assuming you own a set of darts, or a computer to generate random-number picks. If stock prices follow patterns, there is the nagging problem that you will have to be able to recognize these patterns for this insight to do you any good.

To see if this sport is for you, try your hand at the following exercise. In Figures 2C–2F, the final parts of the trends are hidden. Two of these figures are for stocks on the New York Stock Exchange, selected at random. The other two were generated with a short random-walk routine in BASIC; this merely

Figure 2C Real vs. Random Stock-price Patterns

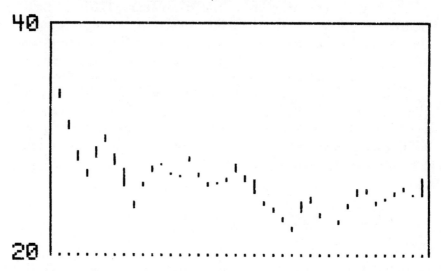

Figure 2D Real vs. Random Stock-price Patterns (*continued*)

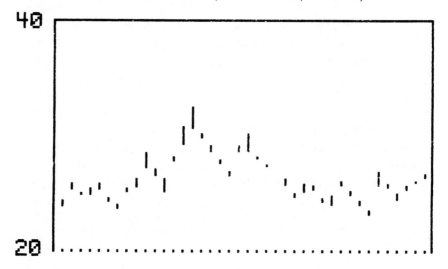

Figure 2E Real vs. Random Stock-price Patterns (*continued*)

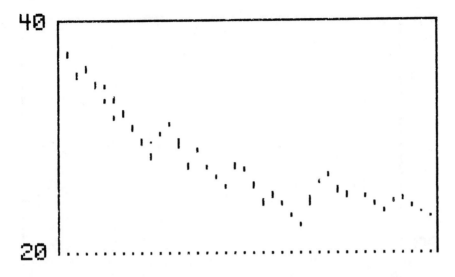

takes a starting price and makes little random jumps up or down for each day. The exercise is to try to guess which figures show the real stocks and then guess which way the price is headed. Ready, set, go!

Figures 2D and 2E show the real stocks. It also happens that Figure 2D's stock is on its way down, dramatically, and Figure 2E's stock is on its way up. Whether you guessed this correctly or not, please read on to determine if you have what it takes to be a market analyst.

Your Life on Wall Street

Imagine for a minute that you are a securities analyst for a large mutual fund (if you are entirely new to this business, a mutual fund is a large stock portfolio, professionally managed, in which you may buy shares whose value goes up or down with the whole portfolio). Every weekday morning, you put

Figure 2F Real vs. Random Stock-price Patterns (*continued*)

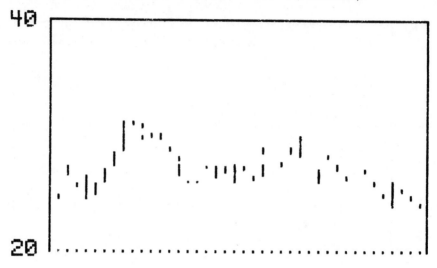

on your three-piece suit and head on down to the office, where you will spend the day studying research reports on various companies and deciding on stock purchases and sales. Almost certainly you will specialize in a particular industry group, such as oil company stocks or electronics. You are going to find your life made difficult by two nagging problems:

- It is a rough business finding stocks that will do well for a long time. As a statistic to contemplate, it happens that of the ten best-performing stocks of 1982, exactly half did better than average and half did worse in 1983. It is typical, in fact, to find that one year's hot stocks are just routine performers in the next year. This suggests pretty coldly that the time scale on which stock behavior is random is a year or less.
- There are all sorts of other analysts out there, working for different companies, and you can't all make money if you all agree all of the time. In fact, when you consider the series of little pushes and pulls on a stock price that occur in the day, most of the larger ones will come from stock purchases and sales authorized by other fund managers whose purpose

in life is to outperform you in the market. There is the haunting and unavoidable suspicion that this competition in guessing future stock prices, carried out by large numbers of people looking at almost the same data, makes the guessing activity itself futile.

So what is the upshot of this effort at prediction and the result of your year of toil over endless documents and hundreds of business lunches? Well, if you have been working for an exceptionally successful fund, you will have outperformed the Standard and Poor average of all stocks by about 20% in sample year 1983 (this was at least a year in which the market was up). If you worked for a less successful fund, your portfolio will have performed about as well as a random selection of stocks. And here, dear reader, is a little fact you should chew on for about a week, especially if you are predisposed to regard with contempt the boring characters who leave their money in banks—a great many funds, a large fraction of all funds, did worse than the market average. All that inside advice, all that constant watching of the ticker tape, all those mornings carefully knotting your tie in the mirror, *All for nothing!* You may reasonably inquire, how is it possible that the study of exponentially-weighted moving averages of stock prices, the study of fundamental factors in an industry, the investigation of the smallest details of particular businesses—how is it possible that these efforts give no more predictive results to trained professionals than flipping a coin? This point will be pondered in a later chapter, in which your computer, immune to your hopes and fears, presents further paradoxes for your delectation. In the meanwhile, please attempt to formulate your own answer.

Performance Statistics

It is time to sharpen up the problem presented above, namely, how can so many experienced, trained professionals generate advice that is utterly worthless? The other side of the problem must also be considered: why do some mutual funds do so much better than others? We will set up a simplified model of funds and portfolios that leads to a few interesting possibilities.

In this model we will assume that there are sixteen possible mutual funds. Furthermore, we will restrict the portfolios of these funds to exactly sixteen stocks. And, as the last restriction, we will require the managers of these funds to pick their stocks at random from the New York Stock Exchange listings.

What do we expect to be the result of this method of stock selection after one year? The most likely outcome, from the rules of probability, would be that most portfolios performed exactly at the market average. In a sampling of sixteen portfolios, one of them is likely to have about four stocks doing better than average and none doing worse (this is taken as cleverness), and one of them should contain four worse-than-average stocks and the rest about average (this is taken as bungling). This would be true whether the market as a whole was up or down for the year; we are just comparing the portfolio stocks to the record of the average stock. (In 1983, for example, the composite index for the New York Stock Exchange rose about 19%. Thus, our average portfolio here would be up 19%, for 1983, anyway).

The results of this portfolio study are summarized in Figure 2G, the interpretation of which is implicitly one of the most crucial points in investment. The crucial point is this— is the man to whom we assigned random portfolio A a genius, and is the man managing random portfolio F a complete dolt? Remember that we assigned these people their baskets of random stocks, and all during the year these people have been going down to their offices every day and pretending to work, possibly reading the Wall Street Journal but more likely checking out the funnies. But what does it mean that portfolio A showed such brilliant market performance? Does this imply that in any year *some* fund will necessarily have outstanding performance compared to other funds? And that the fund managers do not necessarily really know what they are doing?

The answer to this question could be found by picking a favorite hotshot fund and tracking its performance for every year, compared to the market average, over a period of ten to fifteen years. What you would find, not to spoil your suspense or the thrill of the research you may wish to undertake, is that few funds do consistently better than the market average over a time scale of decades. This is why you see ads that proclaim, "The Mississippi Fund outperformed the S&P aver-

Figure 2G The Performance of Random Portfolios

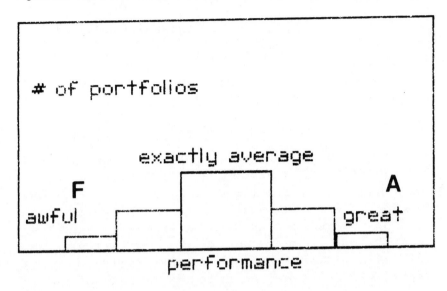

age by 35% from 1979–1981; by 43% from 1980–1982!" The statistics are attempting to swallow this fund's particular hot year, say 1981, and make it appear that an ominous pattern of omniscience is occurring. Alas, such is seldom the case.

It is worth considering what the odds were on a few random propositions. In the jolly rising market of 1983, your chances of doubling your money were about 1 in 20. This is rather surprisingly small, given that the average stock was up almost 20%. The chances of losing half your money, however, were only about 1 out of 150. So if you can't easily make a big killing, at least there is the assurance that you also can't easily be wiped out. There are also two rather large zones of probability for mediocre performance: picking a stock that lost from 0% to 30% had chances of 1 in 5, and picking one that gained from 0% to 15% was also a 1 in 5 bet. All of this data may be summarized in a concept from probability theory called *expectation value*. We will now see how expectation value clarifies the official topic of this chapter, the nature of investment.

Expectation Value and Your Expectations

Expectation value (EV) is really very simple; it is the quantity

$$EV = \text{Payoff} * \text{Probability of Payoff}$$

If you are going to be paid one dollar for correctly calling the roll on a single die, your EV is

$$EV = \$1.00 * (1/6) = \$0.16$$

Thus you should play this game if you can get into it for ten cents and avoid it if it costs a quarter. The stock market, for 1983 at least, has the basic statistic that you expect the average stock to rise 19%; if you were to make up a complex formula based on the possibility of different sizes of gain times the chances of making them (more on this later), you would get an EV of about $270 profit (after commissions) on an investment of $2,000. You may compare this to the simple-minded formulation for a bank time deposit in the same year:

$$EV = (2000 * .09) * 1.00 = \$180$$

In this case the numbers stand for an interest rate of 9% and a probability of 1.00 (1.00 means complete certainty, and after all, the deposit is insured).

The task presenting itself to the investor is to maximize his EV. The reason this is challenging is that the well-known curve shown in Figure 2H approximately represents the relation between risk and payoff. The higher the risk, so the theory goes, the higher the potential profits (there are, of course, numerous hilarious counterexamples of high-risk, low-yield speculations). What this curve really means is, however, that your EV from all types of actions is going to be close to the same—that you will have to pay close attention to sniffing out comparative advantages of a few percent here and a few percent there.

In practice, the way an investment affects your taxes will usually have as much impact on your outcome as the nature of the investment itself. Most of this book will be about finding these comparative advantages and working with them, and a lot of the rest of the book will consist of attempts to discourage you from gambling the family farm on speculative "opportunities." Many investments can be characterized by extremely simple computer models, models that are easy to understand and

Figure 2H Risk vs. Payoff in a Benevolent World

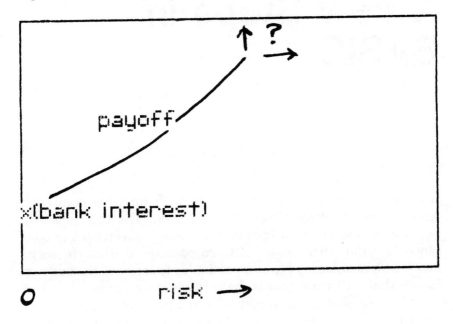

easy to program on the smallest computers, and the thesis expounded here is that you can translate this information into immediate benefits.

3
A Few Steps in BASIC

It is possible to get a great deal of use from your computer without ever writing a line of a program. The pages of any popular computer magazine contain enough advertising to convince you that there is a software package waiting to solve any problem you may have. A particular favorite of the authors is one that will train you to be a fascinating personality and scintillating conversationalist, if you just follow the instructions as they roll off the disk. More serious efforts, however, purport to do every possible financial calculation, from investment planning to detailed stock-market charting.

The idea in this book is that if you are going to be doing some computing relating to your money and your investments, you should use programs that are small enough and clear enough that you understand everything about them. The computer is not magic; it is better at arithmetic than you are and is useful for preparing summaries and tables. There is a tremendous problem in the human tendency to believe that large, complicated pieces of software represent in a mystical way another personality dispensing advice. Large, disk-based stock-charting programs, for example, may seem to be able to predict stock trends. In fact they often fail miserably, which turns out not to be surprising when you have the opportunity to examine the assumptions and simplifications on which the programs are based.

In this book we will spell out all the assumptions first and develop the simplest possible programs, so that things don't appear too magical. As further antimagic, we will also state right now that the amount of BASIC you will need to learn to use this book will be almost embarrassingly little. BASIC was designed, many years ago, to be an easy language for liberal-art-majors to learn. This chapter, which contains 90% of the BASIC ever used in this work, should take you only about two hours to get through even if you hate math and fear keyboards. It should also leave you with the feeling that you are in control of things in financial calculation, a necessary feeling if you are to have confidence in your conclusions.

Step One: Cold Start

There are two standard ways of getting BASIC going on your computer. The simplest home computers usually have BASIC in a ROM chip (read-only memory, a type of permanent memory), so that BASIC is running as soon as the computer is turned on. This approach is sufficiently convenient that as ROM prices drop it is appearing on fancier disk-based systems as well. In the other approach you must load BASIC from a disk. If you have opened your manual at all, you know how to do this by now.

The version of BASIC used in this book has been worked out by taking a standard version of BASIC by Microsoft and then resolutely dropping all features that make it incompatible with BASIC from other suppliers. There will be slight differences in the way the programs appear on the screen from one computer to another, but the programs will work on virtually anything you can buy. This is because nonstandard special features, such as graphics for particular machines, have been avoided.

Your computer will probably give you a bit of screen display identifying the version of BASIC you are using and will display a blinking underline or square, called the *cursor,* to indicate that it is waiting for you to do something. Press in the number 1985, just as you would on a calculator, and then press the Return key (or on some machines, the Enter key). You should see the number on the screen and the blinking space (the cursor) beneath it, waiting to give you another shot. So far so good.

Step Two: The Uses of PRINT

Let's print something, at least in the peculiar sense of printing something on a television screen. None of the programs in this book calls for real printed-on-paper output, but if you are affluent enough to have a printer, the instruction LPRINT instead of PRINT will give you printed output instead of screen output. The way PRINT works is simplicity itself; it looks like this:

    PRINT "(YOUR MESSAGE HERE!)"

You just type in the command PRINT and then enclose the printed message in quotation marks. When you press Return the computer screen displays your message. Here is another remark to try:

    PRINT "MONEY IS IMPORTANT" (press Return)

Your faithful computer should display

    MONEY IS IMPORTANT

Already it's time to address the subject of fallibility. Look around on your keyboard for an "eraser" key such as Del, Backspace, or Rubout. This key will let you erase lines backward as you go. Try typing in

    PRINT "MONEY IS IMPOTENT

and then gobble it all up back to the "IMP" part using whatever key, say Del for consistency, that you have as an eraser. Note that if you press Return (Ret, for short) after typing a fragment such as "PRIN" the computer will come back with "? SYNTAX ERROR" or a similar remark. Some computers have a provision for entering all BASIC keywords, such as PRINT, with a single keystroke. Under these circumstances the Del key will eat the whole word in one chomp.

Try this longer remark:

    PRINT "I LOVE MY COMPUTER AND AM OVERJOYED WITH ITS
    POWER"

(Remember to press Ret.) You will learn two things from this. First, your computer will adjust any message to its display size. If you have a computer with a small display length (the VIC-20 is a prime example), the line above spills over into two lines. Second, it is easier and more error-proof to type short lines than long lines. The programs we will be using have simple enough output that not much line-typing is needed.

Step Three: The Uses of PRINT, Continued

It is also possible to do a little arithmetic with the PRINT statement, and in fact this amounts to using the computer as a pocket calculator. Just to make things challenging, try this sample:

PRINT 2+2 (Ret)

and look for the answer at the top of the screen. To understand a few points, try the following as well:

PRINT 67–33

PRINT 5*9

PRINT 8/9

PRINT 2↑3

The first few small points to note are that an asterisk (*) means "times" and the up arrow (↑) means "to the power of." On some keyboards a little upside-down "v" is used for this (∧), and in a few cases there is a special double asterisk (**). Just check your manual. (For review, 2↑3 means 2*2*2, 4↑5 means 4*4*4*4*4, 10↑2 means 10*10, etc.)

Another point is that computers typically give their numerical results as eight or nine digits, rounded off automatically; consider the case of 8/9, which is really 0.888888888 . . . (with 8s going on forever) but which must be presented in finite form on the computer. This will present a choice in programs about money—you can do some work on output and force the results to show two decimal places, giving answers like PAYMENT = $129.45, or you can write simpler programs that leave the result as PAYMENT = $129.44876 and round off the result when it is copied from the screen to paper. (A few fancy versions of BASIC have a provision for decimal-point positioning in dollars and cents—it's worth checking your manual to see about this.)

The last point in connection with these examples is that the computer will enable you to explore the implications of your money decisions in a more concrete way than has been possible in the past. Can you figure out (1.0+9/1200)↑360 in your head? This sort of computation is easy to get wrong even on a calculator, which typically lets you see only one number at a time rather than a whole expression. Yet this expression has a lot to do with your life if you are sitting on a thirty-year mortgage. With practice in the simple programs in this book, you will begin to feel comfortable with all types of financial calculations.

Step Four: Line Numbers and Running

The PRINT statements above have all been executed in immediate mode, that is, executed as soon as they were entered with Ret. When statements are preceded by a *line number*, they will typically be executed upon entering a RUN instruction. Try this sequence:

```
10 PRINT "HELLO, FRED" (Ret)
RUN
```

When the RUN instruction is entered, the computer looks up all the numbered statements, in this case only one of them, and begins executing them in order. A little variety can be introduced into this situation with the GOTO instruction, which, just as the name implies, tells the computer to go to a numbered line.

Now call this line back onto the screen with the command LIST. LIST is a convenient command and will be used extensively to review and modify programs. If you now type in

```
20 GOTO 10 (Ret)
```

you will see this added to the earlier statement. This little program will execute statement 10 (printing the line) and then execute statement 20, which just tells it to go back to line 10 (and print the same line again). The computer thus fills the screen with its greeting. Some computers will stop when the screen is filled, but most will run on forever, with the last message blinking as an intimation of infinity or perhaps as an intimation of immortality, if such poetic references can be allowed in computing. In that case you need to find either a key marked Stop, Break, or Escape or some other means of interrupting the program. Once more, there are several common ways of doing this and you will have to consult your manual.

Step Five: Closer to Programming

It is time to say good-bye to Fred. You can get rid of this little program with the instruction NEW (or in some cases, CLEAR). Using NEW will always erase whatever program is in the computer, so be careful with it! You should see the cursor come up, as well as a remark such as "READY" or "OK," indicating that your tireless computer is ready for a new challenge.

Now we must get some numbers into the computer, because getting numbers in and out of the computer is basically the topic of this book. Try this small program:

```
10 INPUT A
20 PRINT A
RUN
```

(From now on you will have to remember to press Return after each statement line and after immediate commands such as RUN. It will start to drive you crazy if we list Return after each line.)

What happens? When this program is RUN, the typical computer puts out a question mark to indicate that it is waiting for data. Type in a number and press Return again. The program resumes execution and dutifully prints the number you just entered. In most versions of BASIC, it also leaves the number on the screen as entered. Not too dramatic, but this is the start of more useful things.

One of the advantages of a computer over a calculator is that the computer can put prompts up on the screen to remind you of what the inputs should be. Call the program up using LIST and add (just type these statements in and the friendly computer will put everything in the right order):

```
8 PRINT "APPLES="
20 PRINT "NUMBER OF APPLES =";A
```

Now RUN this package; note that the new statement 20 erases the old one automatically. By the way, it's no wonder that several manufacturers have gone to the trouble of working out a single-keystroke format for commands—you can probably understand how annoying it is to have a long program "bounce" on a computer because you typed IPNUT somewhere instead of INPUT.

When this program is run it should make two points clear: first, it is nice to have the computer ask for numbers by name and to have it label them when they come back out; second, when you use a semicolon in a PRINT statement, the results are printed right next to one another on the same line (try a comma instead of a semicolon and see what difference it makes).

Step Six: Making Life Easier

The substitution of a comma for a semicolon can usually be made very easily using your computer's editing capabilities. Suppose we start with the program of the previous exercise:

```
 8 PRINT "A="
10 INPUT A
20 PRINT "A=";A
```

It is, of course, possible to change the semicolon in line 20 to a comma by typing in a new line 20; that's what had to be done in the previous exercise and for short lines it is not too troublesome. But most computers have a provision for cruising around in the text of your program using the cursor (look for keys on your keyboard with little direction arrows on them). Typically all you have to do is move the cursor around to the position you want changed, type in the new character over the one you want to change, and press Ret. Some computers come with rather fancy editing functions, but these differ so widely from one machine to the next it will have to be the manufacturer's job to explain them.

Although this book is about the rather serious business of money, there is no denying that sailing through program text with the little arrows and editing things with replacements and Del is often lots of fun.

Step Seven: Reality

This next piece of work gets perilously close to real programming. It is a little program that takes an input and squares it, that is, multiplies it by itself. Here is a first version of such a program:

```
10 PRINT "ENTER A NUMBER"
20 INPUT X
30 PRINT "YOUR NUMBER = ";X
40 PRINT "ITS SQUARE IS  ";X*X
```

When you run this program you will probably find that it is a good idea to load programs with reminders about what is going on. There is a special BASIC command called REM (for reminder) for just this purpose, and we could insert the line

```
5 REM THIS PROGRAM SQUARES NUMBERS
```

which would always print out in the program listing but which would be ignored by the computer. Ordinarily, good programming practice demands that REMs be placed in the program to explain any feature that is not entirely obvious. Here, however, we will leave them out to save typing and to conserve computer memory, and program features will be explained in the text. You may consider the whole book to be a giant REM.

In the previous example we were still doing our arithmetic in PRINT statements, but it is now time to get sophisticated. The main arithmetic statement in BASIC is LET, which assigns values. That is,

```
LET A=4
```

assigns the value of 4 to the variable or symbol A, so that if you now were to tell the computer to PRINT A, it would put a 4 up on the screen. The next step up from this simple assignment is the use of LET in arithmetic. If we have already said

```
LET A=4
```

then the statement

```
LET B=2*A
```

will assign the value of 8 to B. These LET statements can be made very complicated, although in this book lines will deliberately be kept short. If you have followed all the information presented up to this point, perhaps it is time to give you the good news that the programs in this book can be of considerable value to you even if you personally don't know that 2*4=8. The computer knows, and that's enough.

The LET statement can be introduced into our current program by adding the line

```
35 LET Z=X*X
```

and changing line 40 to

```
40 PRINT "ITS SQUARE IS ";Z
```

You may run this a few times to convince yourself that this program is functionally the same as the earlier one. A version using this line for squaring:

```
35 LET Z=X↑2
```

would also be the same.

Step Eight: Decisions

The computer can do more than just chug through its program line numbers in sequence, because it has a variety of decision functions. Decisions in BASIC are fairly primitive (there are fancier computer languages, to be sure), and we will be able to get along with IF . . . THEN GOTO for most of this book. For example, it is possible to tack a few statements onto the "squares" program now in the computer to make it more convenient to use. Try adding these lines (call the program up with LIST to get a good look at it):

```
50 PRINT "AGAIN? YES=1,NO=0"
60 INPUT D
70 IF D=1 THEN GOTO 10
80 STOP
```

It's not hard to figure out what this little piece of program is telling the computer to do. The computer tells whoever is running the program that it expects an input; if the input is the number 1, the computer goes back to the top, at line 10, and cooks up another square. Although the program says NO=0, in fact *any* other input will stop the computer because the next line checks to see only if the input D (for *decision*) is the number 1 or not. If you respond to the prompt with "0" the computer will stop, but it will also stop (or in some BASICs, generate an error message) if you feed it a dollar sign or an asterisk or the message "howdy." Give it a few tries and you will discover what sort of error messages your version of BASIC provides; some versions will forgive you all day and keep asking for inputs and some will deal with you harshly.

When you run this program you will see that even tiny programs can begin to give the illusion that you are "talking" to the computer. Only this simple type of decision will be needed to make some of the programs in this book seem fairly friendly and interactive. Part of the problem with very large, "user-friendly" programs is that it is sometimes difficult to remember that what appears on the screen is the canned advice of a potentially fallible programmer, rather than the pronouncement of an oracle.

Step Nine: Over and Over Again

There is actually only one more programming structure with which you should be familiar before applying the programs in this book (you may note by comparing this chapter to your computer manual that all the parts about graphics, plotting, and mathematical functions have been left out—these can be absolutely fascinating, but they have nothing to do with money and thus, crassly, are omitted here). This structure is the one that directs the computer to perform some action repetitively. After all, to a certain extent what makes computers valuable is their willingness to crank through the same boring calculations over again. If you still have the old program in the computer, enter NEW to clear it and try this fragment:

```
10 FOR N=1 TO 10
20 PRINT N
30 NEXT N
```

Run it and see what happens. Although most of the microcomputers used these days can work this out in about a millisecond, some of them have such slow display management that the computer appears to be counting like a four-year-old. Others fill the screen so fast it looks like it's exploding. *Anything* you have bought will be plenty fast enough for the calculations we will be doing.

A variation of this program may be obtained by replacing line 20 with another one:

```
20 PRINT "LET'S DO THIS TEN TIMES"
```

What happened to "N" in this example? It is simply used as a counter, and because we don't ask the computer to do anything with it, it doesn't show up in the output. Try sticking this back in the program:

```
15 PRINT N
```

and running the program again (among other things this shows how many times that statement was printed). As a further slight variant, erase statement 20, by typing 20 and pressing Ret, and insert this:

```
15 PRINT N,N*N
```

When the program is run it prints a nice little table of squares.

Believe it or not, with this rather modest background you are now ready to set forth into the world of financial programming. Although it may not be sporting to tell you this so far in advance, what you will find is that most calculations in this area can be done very easily, thanks to the computer. Rather fancy operations, such as stock-market simulation, will turn out to be quick work in a short program. The idea here is that perhaps you will want to learn a little more about programming if programming does you any good, for example, if it saves you some money.

BASIC for Finance, a Very Short Course

Most of the calculations undertaken here will involve straightforward use of standard formulas that have been known in financial practice for centuries. These calculations can be done with specialized "business" calculators on which the little keys are labelled "PMT," "FV," "i," and so forth. We will present a review of these calculations, noting the advantages of doing this work in BASIC—on even a small computer—rather than using a financial calculator. These advantages are

• The computer can be programmed to ask for needed information in a readily recognized way. It will ask for inputs as words, such as "TOTAL LOAN AMOUNT," instead of expecting you to know which lump of money is "FV" in each kind of problem.

- The computer is flexible. For example, if you have a financial calculator, what do you think you should do to calculate the real return on savings at 9% when the inflation rate is 11%? (Hint: you can't do it first at nine and then at 11 and divide the answers.) Yet this situation is no problem at all to handle in a BASIC program, and once more all you have to understand is the meaning of the problem, not the equations.
- The computer can present different cases for easy comparison on the screen at the same time. The single-number display on even expensive business calculators is truly unhelpful in this regard.

This section will cover a few standard situations, showing how financial formulas are derived. Later in the book, some formulas will appear in programs without much explanation, on the assumption that the reader is probably more immediately concerned about money than about mathematics. What will rapidly become clear in all these situations is that only a few simple routines are needed to cover all types of finance; banks have definitely figured out how they like to do business.

The Starting Point: Compound Interest

Simple interest is beneath the dignity of your computer, because it represents a single multiplication performed only once. If you borrow $2,000 at 8% simple interest for one year, at the end of the year you owe the original $2,000 plus $160, which is 8% of $2,000 (0.08 * 2,000). If you can pardon such a horrid pun, this situation is not very interesting. Thus, compound interest was born.

The standard modification of the situation involving the $2,000 above might be that instead of simple interest, the 8% will be taken as a nominal annual 8%, compounded monthly. This means that the 8% is divided into twelve little chunks, as

8% = 0.08 annual
0.08/12 = 0.0066667 monthly.

In the simple interest case, the total amount owed at the end of the loan period was

$$\text{total} = \$2,000 * (1 + 0.08)$$
$$= \$2,000 + \$160 = \$2,160.$$

In this case, the same formula is used, except on a monthly basis, and in each succeeding month the interest term will apply to the original $2,000 as well as to the smaller interest term. The schedule goes this way:

First month: total = $2,000 * (1 + .0066667) = $2,013.33

Second month: total = $2,013.33 * (1 + .0066667) = $2,026.76

Third month: total = $2,026.76 * (1 + .0066667) = $2,040.27

and so on, for twelve months.

This is clearly a case for a little program. We will stick to the specific numbers at hand for the moment and then work up a general example. We will generate the month totals using a variable Z that is the quantity (1 + .0066667) listed above; we also will step through the multiplication using a counter called K, which is to run from 1 to 12 in the FOR . . . NEXT loop. For reasons lost in the mists of time, the counters in this book will almost always be K or M.

```
10 LET A = 2000
20 LET I = 0.08/12
30 LET Z=(1+I)
40 FOR K=1 TO 12
50 LET A = A*Z
60 NEXT K
70 PRINT "TOTAL OWED = $";A
```

This should show a total owed of $2,165.999, which your lender will undoubtedly be willing to round off to $2,166. It is always possible to round off these dollar totals on the computer, but at the cost of putting in three or four lines of fussy output typing; we are therefore going to round off by hand (really, it will be less work). The point to note here is that the interest works out to be more than it was in the simple interest example because of the monthly compounding. In this case the difference is only six dollars—for longer time periods and higher interest rates the effect of compounding is much more impressive.

The program above gives as its answer the quantity A, which was the original A multiplied by Z twelve times. The compact notation for this quantity on the computer would be the expression $A*(Z\uparrow12)$, or A times the quantity (Z to the power 12). Let's stick in this patch at the end of the existing program:

```
80 STOP
90 LET A=2000*(Z↑12)
100 GOTO 70
```

Run the program again and then run this part of the program by typing in GOTO 90. What happens? The same answer appears, because the two statements are equivalent. (This is a tribute to the numerical accuracy of your computer; on many calculators the results would not be identical.)

The calculation above turns out to be this formula from the financial handbooks:

$$FV = PV * (1 + I)\uparrow N$$

or, as it actually appears in those works:

$$FV = PV * (1 + i)^n$$

This expression contains four of the five quantities that comprise the whole universe of finance (the other one is PMT, or payment, and will appear shortly). Here is a short introduction to these ubiquitous variables:

FV Future value of an amount of money. If you borrowed the money, the future value is the $2,166 that you have to pay. If you had deposited the $2,000 in a bank for 8% compounded monthly, the future value, $2,166, is what your deposit will be worth.

PV Present value of an amount of money. That's the $2,000 in the example above. In a mortgage calculation, PV is the amount you are trying to get from the bank (FV is what you will end up paying over the years).

N Number of time intervals for compounding. It's 12 in this example because we compounded monthly for a year. Banks can get very precise about this, compounding daily and taking leap years into account.

▮ Interest rate, specifically the rate per compounding period. That's why 8%/12 is used instead of 8% in this example.

The Next Step: Payments Plus Interest

Regular payments introduce one more level of complication into these calculations, but it really isn't too difficult. Suppose you had the $2,000 above and were putting it in a bank to earn the 8% interest. We will change the interest rules and your finances to go like this: every year you will take $2,000 on December 31 and put it in the bank, and the bank will pay 8% per year, but not compounded monthly. This routine will go on for twenty years. How much money will you have at the end of the twenty years? We can run up the beginning of this computation by hand to see how a program might work:

> First Year: $2,000 (deposited last day of year; no interest)
> Next Year: $2,000 * (1 + 0.08) + $2,000
> Next Year: $2,000 * (1 + 0.08) * (1 + 0.08) + $2,000 * (1 + 0.08) + $2,000

In the first year there is just the payment itself; in the next year there is that year's payment, plus last year's with its interest. By the third year the original deposit has been sitting around for two interest periods, last year's has picked up one round of interest, and there is, of course, the current year's deposit. This is something of a nuisance to work out by hand, but two convenient escapes from drudgery appear: first, this is a simple computer problem, and second, there is an algebraic formula that takes into account these repeated interest multiplications.

The program is fairly tidy and just steps through the sequence shown. Try typing this in:

```
10 LET AMT=2000
20 LET Z=(1+0.08)
30 LET SUM=AMT
40 FOR K=1 TO 19
50 LET AMT=AMT*Z
```

```
60 LET SUM=SUM+AMT
70 NEXT K
80 PRINT "TOTAL = $";SUM
```

If you are interested in programming, you should step this through a few cycles and see that it really does what it should. (If you're not interested in programming, you can skip this whole chapter anyway with no adverse consequences.)

Running the program should give the result $91,523.929, more or less; different versions of BASIC use different round-off routines. You may have noticed, by the way, the overwhelming resemblance between the scheme outlined here and the basic savings-and-loan IRA (individual retirement account).

The algebraic formula for this same situation is:

$$FV = PMT*((1+I) \uparrow N - 1)/I$$

For this example, PMT is the $2,000, N is 20 and I is 0.08, meaning 8%. If you append this formula to the program as

```
90 LET SUM=2000*((Z↑20)−1)/0.08
100 PRINT SUM
```

and run it by typing GOTO 90, you will see the same answer, give or take a few cents.

There will be some occasions on which it is possible to do interesting things with a FOR . . . NEXT loop, and then other occasions on which it will be better to use the algebraic method to condense the computation to a single line. Usually, in this book, the choice of calculation method will be made on the basis of ease of program entry rather than mathematical elegance.

The Last Word: Regular Payments

The expressions in lines 90–100 above can be combined to give one line that tells what PMT (your payments) will be, in terms of PV (the amount of money you are trying to borrow). It's really quite simple as an algebra problem; just equate the two different forms above for FV and you are left with an equation that contains PMT on one side and PV, N, and I on the other. What emerges is

$$PMT = PV*I/(1-(1+I) \uparrow (-N))$$

which may be incorporated into a small program to run the now-famous problem of the $2,000 as a monthly payment example. The program is

```
10 PRINT "INPUT AMT, N, I"
20 INPUT PV
30 INPUT N
40 INPUT I
50 LET PMT=PV*I/(1−(1+I)↑(−N))
60 PRINT "PMT = $";PMT
```

This is a stripped-down version of nicer programs that won't require you to know much about how they work. In this case you have to run our example by responding to the INPUT prompt with

2000 (Ret)
0.08/12 (Ret)
12 (Ret)

because the appropriate interest rate is the montly interest and the number of compounding terms is 12. You should be rewarded for your labors by the answer

PMT=$173.98

or so, which corresponds to yearly payments of $2,087.72. This is less than the total in wait-to-the-end-of-the-year mode of payment because not all of the money is out at interest for the whole year.

Saving Your Work

Most of the programs in the next section of the book are either variations or extensions of the easy BASIC programs just presented. There are a few new tricks, such as the DIM statement and random-number functions, but we will explain these as we go along. The way to use this book is to find a topic about which you are curious, read the chapter, and then type in the program or programs of interest at the time. The idea is to get an understanding of a few important topics, with programs short enough that they take only a few minutes to type in. If you then save the programs on tape or disk, you will have a collection personalized to your own financial concerns. Remember, what you should get from this experience ultimately is some kind of intuition about the standard financial deals available in this society; this is safer than relying on someone else's assumptions-in-software to steer you straight.

Saving Your Sanity

There are just a few final points to be mentioned in connection with the PRINT statement. You will notice, as you proceed through the book that the usual way of inputting numbers looks like this:

```
100 PRINT "AMOUNT"
150 INPUT A
200 PRINT A
```

This makes the computer prompt you for the number (line 100), then output a question mark to indicate that it is waiting for the input. In some systems, the number you input will appear on the screen and stay there. In that case, you don't need line 200. Virtually all the programs in the book have all three lines; you may find that this drives you crazy if your particular computer then puts input on the screen twice (you'll see what we mean when you try a few programs). The solution is simple enough—just delete the lines in which PRINT follows INPUT immediately.

You may have a printer as well, in which case you may want to do versions of the programs in which PRINT has been replaced by LPRINT. You probably already know this if you have done a few BASIC programs, but if you have been running only packaged software, you might not.

4
Your Taxes

It's time to focus our attention on the IRS. This highly esteemed organization has occasionally been irreverently referred to by a mammoth list of names that could not comfortably be printed in a family book. Irrespective of which euphemism you prefer, most people agree that taxes are taking a big bite out of most people's paychecks, and the recent trend in legislation has been to put more teeth into the laws that insist that those bites be taken. As you begin your climb toward financial stability, it is imperative to learn the basic ins and outs of the tax game, the sport in which the entire country actively, if not willingly, participates.

The tax game hasn't always been this popular. Until 1913, except for a few years of temporary insanity, the United States didn't even have an income tax. Then Congress discovered that accountants had come up with a concept called *income;* the senators and representatives figured that, because the word was in the dictionary, it should be taxed. So they passed a constitutional amendment making possible the agony of defeat (without much joy of victory) with which we have all become so familiar.

As usual, it all started innocently enough. There was effectively a standard deduction that eliminated the solid majority of the population from paying *any* tax. Most of those people who did get hit by the tax paid a whopping 1%, and that's *not* a typographical error. Only those with taxable income over $20,000—and in 1913, these were really the rich folks—became familiar with "brackets"; income over $20,000 was hit with a 2% tax. You really had something to complain about if you pulled in over half a million dollars a year: you had reached the 7% bracket! In retrospect, this may appear miniscule, but at the time the wealthy considered it an outrage.

In some measure, we really can't complain today. There have been times when a 90% bracket was achieved. Now the most you'll have the privilege of paying is 50%. Of course, with the "bracket creep" of inflationary times, more and more countrymen have been achieving this honored status each year.

Effects of Graduation

Before getting into "bracket creep," it's essential to discuss the plain-vanilla "bracket." It's amazing how many misconceptions people have about what their actual tax bracket is, especially with fancy "tax tables" and fancier accountants shielding people from such mundane matters. A lot of folks think that they can divide their tax liability by their taxable income, or some other "income" number, and, *violà*, that's the bracket. Not so. Even worse, we have dealt with people who think they don't even have *any* tax bracket as long as they get a refund each April. Have we ever got news for them!

Our tax structure is based on a "graduated" system. This basically means that the more you make, the more your *next* dollar will be taxed. The corollary is that the more you make, the more tax will be *saved* by your next deduction. In effect, in 1984 each single person can have a taxable income of $3,300 tax-free. Most Americans would consider trying to live on this sum to be constraining, to say the least. The next $1,100 you make is taxed at a rate of 11%. Thus on the *first* $4,400 a year you pull in, if you're happily unmarried, you will pay a tax of $121 (11% of 1,100); this is true for that first $4,400 even if there's another million dollars of income in the wings waiting to be hit with taxes.

There is a notion making its way around the country that some raises should be turned down, because they bump you into a higher tax bracket and actually reduce the amount of money you have left over. This probably originated as a distortion of the tale of woe that can befall those who stand to lose "transfer payments," such as Welfare or Social Security, when they earn a salary. Although this often happens, the distorted version holds that people who are not receiving transfer payments could suffer a similar fate. *This is a mistake!* The only money that would be taxed in a higher bracket is that next dollar; your previous net is still your own money. Because the old "net" is "safe," one accountant we know refers to this amount as a "safety net"; because this sort of humor is somewhat typical among accountants, you can understand why no reasonable people invite them to parties.

The fellow may desperately lack a sense of humor, but the point is still valid. If you learn nothing else from this book, remember this: until we reach that glorious day when the tax rate bounds over 100%, tote that barge, lift that bale, and take that raise.

Knowing Your Bracket

There are several ways to find out what your own federal tax bracket is. One is to understand the structure of the "Tax Rate Schedules" well enough to be able to pull the rate out of them, as most accountants can do at a glance. Another way is to pay a CPA to tell you, although if you're a good client (that is, if your account with him is fully paid), he'll probably do it as a courtesy. Another way, of course, is to enter and run the central program of this chapter.

This program is the first of several that will be developed one piece at a time. Depending upon the efficiency of your computer, it could require as much as 5K (about 5,000 "bytes") of memory, but with the cost of memory these days, most home computers should be able to handle that with the greatest of ease.

Also please note that the typing involved in entering this program is significantly more than for most other programs in this book. You can thank the government for adding complexities to life; the other programs are based on logic, and are thus much less contorted.

The first logical step is to program the tax rate schedules into the computer. For this, we'll have to get a bit more sophisticated and program with such spiffy tools as arrays and data statements. If you want to show the world that you're with it in the silicon era, you would refer to this as "manipulating data."

Because a program that just loads itself with the tax rate schedules and has no input or output is remarkably boring to run, we'll spice it up by having it actually calculate a tax. That way, you can confirm that it's really alive and well. We'll start with the outline, excluding the actual schedule numbers at first. Type Program 4A in for starters and save it on tape or disk.

PROGRAM 4A
Generic Tax Calculator

```
50 DIM X(20), Y(20), Z(20)
100 GOSUB 10000
150 PRINT "WHAT IS TAXABLE INCOME?"
200 INPUT I
210 PRINT I
250 GOSUB 12050
300 PRINT "INCOME TAX: $";T
9950 STOP
10000 FOR N=1 TO 100
10050 READ A
10100 READ B
10150 READ C
10200 LET X(N)=A
10250 LET Y(N)=B
10300 LET Z(N)=C
10350 IF A=999999 THEN 10450
10400 NEXT N
10450 RETURN
10500 DATA 0,0,.00
11950 DATA 999999,0,.5
12000 IF I<1 THEN I=1
12050 FOR M=1 TO N−1
12100 IF I<=X (M) THEN 12250
12150 NEXT M
12200 LET M=M−1
12250 IF X(M)=999999 THEN M=M−1
12300 LET T=(I−X(M−1))*Z(M)+Y(M)
12900 RETURN
```

Don't bother trying to run this program quite yet. If you do, you'll discover that it will tell you that you live in a wonderful society in which you pay absolutely no tax, regardless of your income. Reality notwithstanding, let's look at what we have already.

Arrays and Subroutines

This program has enough new BASIC statements to warrant a bit of explanation. The DIM statement in line 50 won't turn down the lights; that's just BASIC for "DIMension," and it says how many different values can be stored in the arrays X(), Y(), and Z(). What's an *array?* you astutely inquire.

Well, you've regularly been playing with *variables*, which are the letters floating around in earlier programs in this book and in *Basic Money*. These letters act as surrogates for numbers, taking on whatever values we tell them to have. Arrays are pretty much the same thing, except that each array can take on a slew of values and remember all of them. What's a slew? As big as you want it to be, within the limits of your computer's capabilities. How do you tell the computer how big you want a slew to be? With the DIM statement. Thus, in this partial program, we've told the computer to save enough room to be able to store up to 20 values for each of the three arrays. These arrays are for storing the three columns of numbers in the tax-rate schedules.

Before the arrays are useful, we have to fill them with appropriate numbers. This is the function of the lines starting at 10000, and "called" in line 100. The GOSUB there is just BASIC's way of taking a temporary detour to do some instructions in another part of the program before continuing upon its merry way. These detours are commonly called *subroutines*.

Lines 10000 through 10400 are a familiar FOR . . . NEXT loop, with a new twist or two. The first time through, the READ statement in line 10050 gives A the value found in the first DATA statement anywhere in the program. Line 10100 assigns the next value found into B, and line 10150 plops the next one into C. After the first time through the loop, values in subsequent DATA statements are put into these same variables.

Unfortunately, when this happens, the prior value is forgotten unless we put it into another variable. Arrays make marvelous receptacles for this sort of data, which brings us to the purpose of lines 10200 through 10300. These lines assign the values from A, B, and C respectively to the next available cell, or *element,* of the X(), Y(), and Z() arrays.

Because a prescribed length for tax tables is not (yet) part of the tax law, we have to devise some means of determining that we've reached the end of the data. Otherwise we would continue the FOR . . . NEXT loop 100 times, and the poor computer would suffer miserably trying to read data that just isn't there. Under these circumstances, most BASICs respond by politely telling you that you've asked for the impossible, so the language simply stops trying to execute the program. Thus we set a value of 999999 to be read into variable A to indicate that we want to get out of the loop. Line 10350 looks for the indicator; when it is found, the program jumps past the end of the loop, which ends with the standard NEXT in line 10400.

Arrays are tremendously powerful tools in BASIC, and a truly thorough treatment of them is beyond the scope of this tome. *BASIC and the Personal Computer* by Dwyer and Critchfield (Reading, MA: Addison-Wesley, 1978) is a good choice among the vast number of books readily available to teach you to employ the full power of these structures.

The RETURN in line 10450 tells BASIC that the detour started by the GOSUB at line 100 has ended, and the flow of the program should return to line 150. Omission of this statement in a subroutine could cause your BASIC to float eternally down the "river of no RETURN."

Lines 10500 through 11950 are reserved for the rate schedule data. A glance at the listing will show you that the table you've entered this time around is pretty minimal; the second DATA line is the end of the whole thing, as indicated by the 999999 value. The first one sets up a tax bracket of zero for all income over zero. This table is appropriate for people who don't file returns and who assume that the IRS will never catch up with them. We do not recommend extensive use of it.

Now that the subroutine has built a tax table into the arrays, which is a form BASIC can comfortably use, the program can calculate a tax after the user supplies the taxable income. Another subroutine—at line 12000—is invoked to actually calculate the taxes based on the tables and the taxable income.

Line 12000 makes sure that there actually *is* a taxable income, to keep the computer's sanity intact. Then the FOR . . . NEXT loop from lines 12050 through 12150 finds the part of the arrays that handles income just a bit higher than the one that was specified. Line 12200 is used to back up one notch in the arrays, correcting for the overshot, and line 12250 makes sure we're not at the artificial "highest" bracket, indicated by the 999999 flag. Such contortions could have been avoided by using another array, but that would mean more typing to put in the data statements. From experience, we have discovered that more typing leads to more errors and frustrations; we despise both of these consequences.

To work well, this program should have some tables. Because there are four different tables for individuals each year and because we assume you'd rather not type in any more than the minimum you can get away with, we will use a partial table for a couple of examples, showing you as we do it how to construct the data statements you need straight from the tables that the IRS, in its generosity, sends to you gratis each year.

Taxable Income—What Is It?

Before you can use these tables, you have to be able to answer the one question the program poses: what is taxable income? Although the program wants you to enter a number, you have to understand the question in the general sense . . . what *is* taxable income?

The simplest answer is that taxable income is, for 1983, the number on line 37 of your form 1040 (long form), a document with which everyone is at least remotely acquainted. The lines tend to move around from year to year, but the "taxable income" label is consistent.

The somewhat more intellectually useful definition is gross income, minus some adjustments (such as IRA deductions and special deductions for working couples), minus "excess" itemized deductions, minus exemption deductions. This is the skeleton of the "great 1040." We'll ignore the possibility that you have made a few charitable contributions but didn't itemize; the deduction is common, but sufficiently miniscule to be more trouble than it's worth for our purposes.

A brief explanation of *itemized deductions,* and how to figure if they're worthwhile for you to submit on April 15, is in order. Those of us over 25 are accustomed to hearing about the *standard deduction.* The idea was to get more itemized deductions than the standard, put them on Schedule 1040 A, and smile proudly at your lesser friends who didn't.

The concept remains, but the vocabulary and contortions have changed, becoming somewhat less intuitive. The standard deduction has been replaced by the *Zero-Bracket Amount,* or ZBA. The tax rate schedules have all been adjusted to reflect the ZBA as a starting point; the schedules used to start at $0, but everyone got a standard deduction before even going to them. In the "old days," itemized deductions were simply deducted; now you deduct only "excess itemized deductions," which represent the amount by which your itemized deductions exceed the ZBA. Despite these contortions, the end result hasn't really changed. By the way, in case you hadn't guessed, the bill that enacted these cosmetic alterations is referred to as the Tax Reduction and Simplification Act. Really.

What do itemized deductions include? Generally speaking, they are personal expenses that Congress has seen fit to give a tax preference. The main instigation is lobbying groups for industries. Thus medical bills are partially deductible, but only to the extent that they exceed a percentage of your gross income. Most state and local taxes qualify. Most interest paid, highlighted by that on your home mortgage, is an itemized deduction. Charitable contributions are in the select group too, as are accountants' fees, union dues and, generally, "all ordinary and necessary expenses paid or incurred . . . for the production or collection of income; for the management, conservation or maintenance of property held for the production of income; or in connection with the determination, collection, or refund of any tax." Those words are straight from the Internal Revenue Code, which is the tax law.

Note them diligently. If you bought this book to learn to produce more income, or to learn more about how to approach life in a world that includes taxes, your cost can be included as one of the "miscellaneous itemized deductions" in Schedule A.

How about your computer itself? To the extent that you bought and use it for investment and tax-related purposes, it's indirectly deductible. The "indirect" part relates to depreciation, which means you get to deduct it over a period of time. Depreciation and such other matters will be covered more thoroughly in later chapters, but keep in mind that you *may* be able to get some of your computer expenditure back from the

U.S. government. We'll touch on the ramifications of the 1984 Tax Reform Act at the end of this chapter.

Tax Case the First: What Bracket To Use?

Now you've got enough of an idea of what's going on to analyze the plights of a couple of hypothetical individuals. If Program 4A is not in memory now, reload it from disk or tape; then, to play along with the examples, type in the BASIC statements that follow.

First consider the case of Sally Single. She has advanced to middle management in a consulting firm and earned $35,125 in 1983. She is unmarried and lives in Texas, a state that imposes no income taxes on individuals. She rents an apartment in Houston for $850 a month. Alas, not only does she have no spouse to share her tax burden, she also does not even have enough deductions to itemize. She has $2,000 left over to invest for a ten-year period and is debating between investing it in a bank Certificate of Deposit (CD) yielding 12% or a municipal bond fund offering 8%. She has decided against an IRA, thinking that she just might want to spend a week in Bermuda next year, and the IRA premature-distribution penalties would be too steep.

Her taxable income is simple enough to figure. There aren't any adjustments to gross income or excess itemized deductions to contend with. All that's necessary is to subtract her exemption deduction of $1,000 from her gross wages, leaving a taxable income of $34,125. Note that the amount of effort on her part to "earn" the exemption deduction was to be alive at some point during the taxable year.

Her taxes are pretty simple to figure, too, especially with a computer handy. The applicable portion of the 1983 Tax Rate Schedule X, which is the one single people use, looks like Table 4A.

Because we're looking at 1983 taxable income, we'll use the data in this table to construct data statements for Sally. Remember that we need three numbers for each line in the table, to fill the three arrays we've set up. There are five numbers on each line, but a very quick glance shows that the right-hand column is identical to the left-hand column. Furthermore, the second column from the left duplicates the first one, except

Table 4A Applicable Portion of 1983 Tax Rate Schedule for Sally Single

If the amount on Form 1040, line 37 is	But not over	Enter on Form 1040, line 38	Of the amount over
28,800	34,100	6,045 + 36%	28,800
34,100	41,500	7,953 + 40%	34,100
41,500	55,300	10,913 + 45%	41,500

that everything is shifted one notch up. Our aversion to typing inspired us to let the computer do the duplicating in the program. Only the second column and the two values in the third column need to be typed in. The following BASIC statements do the trick.

PROGRAM 4B
Sally Single's Tax-schedule Data

```
11050 DATA 34100,6045, . 36
11100 DATA 41500,7953, . 40
11150 DATA 55300,10913, . 45
```

Look at the first line in Table 4A and then look at line 11050. The BASIC lines are simply a line number followed by the BASIC word DATA and the numbers from the second and third columns of the published tax rate schedule. The line numbers used must be somewhere between 10550 and 11900. Furthermore, they must be in the same order as the values of the schedule. It is the nature of BASIC to organize the things you enter by line numbers; the sequence in which you actually type the lines is ignored.

The values after DATA are separated by commas. If you want to get strange results, you could type "$34,100" as "34,100" instead of "34100"; BASIC will assume you meant to enter two numbers—34 and 100—instead of a single value. The only guarantee we give you is that answers you get using this form of data entry will be wrong.

Also, because the second values in the third column of the table are percentages, they should be preceded by a decimal point (a period on your keyboard) to reflect their true nature.

How can you determine which lines from the rate schedule are appropriate? Just enter the values from the line reflecting the taxable income in question, as well as the data from the preceding and the following lines. Of course, you can be certain of getting the right information in by typing data statements for the entire schedule, but such drudgery should be avoided whenever possible.

Before running this program, recall that when answering a question from BASIC, you must again scrupulously avoid including the commas within the value. When you input a taxable income of "$12,345," tell the computer "12345."

If you enter the lines with the data statements and run the program, using $34,125 ("34125") for taxable income, you will notice that Sally's tax is $7,963. This agrees completely with the Tax Tables, that mammoth set of figures that clutters up about six pages of the tax-return packages each year. This correlation lends credibility to the accuracy of the typing.

But if you assume that Sally had made $25 less, or $24 dollars more, you wind up with a tax of $7,953 or $7,973, respectively. The table still says $7,963. The reason for this $10 discrepancy is that the tables use taxable income "give or take" $25, rather than the calculated precision your computer gave you. In a sense, your computer is more accurate than the tables; at least, it's more precise.

Of course, Sally already knew her liability; her local street-corner tax preparer had pointed that out to her when he told her that the balance due on that liability was $3,456. Being a bright and educated person, she did not make classic error number one: focusing on her balance due (or on her refund) rather than her total tax liability. She is aware that the balance due is as dependent on the withholding and estimated taxes that she has already paid as it is on the actual tax she pays.

As an aside, we know of some accountants who shield their clients from this basic bit of wisdom. The idea is that the accountant is then free to encourage the unsuspecting client to pay an unnecessarily large amount in withholding and estimated taxes. Then, next April, when the dust settles, there is a fat refund. The poor client, ignoring the tax liability involved, becomes convinced that the refund is due to the accountant's genius in preparing the return. Of course, it was really due to the taxpayer's generosity in using the government for his "savings," without earning any interest. It is imperative to understand that *large refunds are not always desirable;* they reflect unproductive investment of funds as often as they reflect real, effective cuts in taxes paid.

Sally was already aware of this and, having some mathematical instinct, analyzed her investment alternatives based on this knowledge. She figured that in each year of the prospective ten-year investment period, the CD yielding 12% would give her interest of $240, and the tax-free munis would give her only $160. Realizing that the CD is taxable, though, she fell into classic error number two. She pulled out her pocket calculator and figured that her tax rate was $7,963 divided by $34,125, or 23.3%. Thus she expected her tax on the CD to be 23.3% of the $240 interest, or $56, each year; this would give her a net profit of $184 a year, which would beat the $160 the munis yielded by $240 over the ten-year period.

Classic error? Recall that this chapter began with an emphasis on your *real* tax bracket, as contrasted with the perceived bracket. A small modification to the program will give the needed information. With programs 4A and 4B still in memory, add the following lines:

PROGRAM 4C
Tax-bracket Calculator

```
350 PRINT "AVG BRACKET: ";V*100;"%, BUT"
400 PRINT "REAL BRACKET: ";B*100;"%"
450 PRINT "IF INCOME DROPS BY $";I-L
500 PRINT "REAL BRACKET: ";D*100;"%"
550 PRINT "IF INCOME RISES BY $";H-I
600 PRINT "REAL BRACKET: ";C*100;"%"
12350 B=Z(M)
12400 V=INT(T/I*1000+.5)/1000
12450 H=X(M)
12500 C=Z(M+1)
12550 L=X(M-1)
12600 D=Z(M-1)
```

Be sure, as always, to save this revised version of the tax calculator on tape or disk. This modification will give a lot more information than just the amount of the tax. If you run it, again using taxable income of $34,125, you will see that the average bracket is 23.3%. This is the rate Sally had calculated. The *real* bracket, however, is shown as 40%. This is a significant difference. It also points out that, if her income dropped by a mere $25 (and one cent, really), her bracket would go down to 36%; another $7,375 would bump her into the 45% bracket.

Could the computer be right? Sally expects that if her income goes up by $240, her tax would go up by $56, to $8,019. The computer is saying that the tax increase would be 40% of $240, or $96, which would bring the total to $8,059. Give it the test—run the program again, using taxable income of $34,365, representing the old income plus the $240 interest. The tax is $8,059. She is indeed in a 40% bracket.

Does this change the investment picture? With a tax of $96 on the CD, her yield is just $144. Now the muni beats it by $160 over the ten years; contrast this with her conclusion above.

The moral of this little exercise is that faulty perception of your tax bracket can quickly lead to wrong decisions, which in turn can cause you to lose money. In many of the programs throughout this book, you will need to have some idea of what your tax bracket is. *Use the real bracket rather than the average.*

This simple analysis also points out one other concern, which will be examined more fully in Chapter 9. The key to tax considerations in analyzing any sort of investment is to focus on net-of-tax return, not the number of dollars of tax saved. If saving taxes is your only goal, quit your job. Your taxes will promptly drop. Along with your standard of living.

We looked at Sally's 1983 picture. Would things change in different years? Of course. The line numbers on the 1040 change with the whims of the IRS; the dollar amounts and percentages are subject to the climate in Washington. But the basic idea, and the bulk of the program, should remain valid for years. Only the data statements should have to be changed, and you know how to construct them.

The Truth Revealed

However, before you invest time and effort in typing in data statements from the tax rate schedules for your own taxes, allow us to reveal the hidden truth about the real bracket. You may recall that we mentioned earlier that a "trained" ac-

countant can tell what your tax bracket is at a glance. Now
that you've seen how the data statements were constructed,
you are equally "trained." Note that, in the partial tax-rate
schedule used to create Sally Single's data statements, the percentage shown in the third column of the line for income between $34,100 and $41,500 in the rate schedule is 40%. Sally's
real tax bracket is 40%.

This is not a coincidence. Line 12350 in Program 4C simply
extracted that value from the array and put it into variable
B (as in "Bracket"). B was massaged a bit to make it look
like a percent instead of a decimal value; then it was displayed
as the real bracket.

So now you know the awful truth; the "trained" accountant
who can tell you your bracket at a glance is simply trained
in reading a number from a tax schedule.

Does this mean that the program you've typed in is useless?
Not at all. First of all, it's a handy little tax calculator, adaptable
readily to different years and filing statuses, at least until Congress changes some of the laws so drastically that this whole
approach no longer applies. This would be true, for example,
if a flat-rate tax were passed into law. By the way, this proposal
has come up regularly since 1913. It hasn't passed yet.

Tax Case the Second: Income Averaging

In addition to being a handy tax calculator (and an impressive
display for your neighbors, showing off both your tax and programming expertise), the program is also useful as a good start
on an income-averaging calculator.

Income averaging has been one of the most useful as well
as one of the most misunderstood gimmicks available to the
beleaguered tax-paying citizen. And it can have a significant
effect on your real bracket.

It is a direct outgrowth of the graduated tax system. Some
people have income that fluctuates significantly from year to
year. These people suffer unmercifully in a graduated tax system. To use an extreme case, consider the single Frank Farmer,
who barely managed to survive for four straight years; he
earned exactly $4,500 in taxable income. His annual tax bill
was $266, and he lived in a real bracket of 15%. During those
first four years, one could say that he had a terrific tax shelter,

but abject poverty has been an effective tax dodge since the Egyptians analyzed sources of funds for the pyramids.

In the fifth year, a banner harvest resulted in a taxable income of $34,125, the same amount Sally Single earned as a successful executive. As we've already figured, the 1983 tax on this is $7,963, which puts Farmer in a 40% bracket along with other people who eke out a decent living. But does he really belong there? His total income over the five years is only $52,125, an average of $10,425 per year. With the graduated system, his five-year tax tab comes to $9,027. If he had earned $10,425 each year instead of sporadically, his tax would only be $1,193 per year, or $5,965 over the five-year period. That's a difference of $3,062, constituting cruel and unusual punishment for people with fluctuating fortunes.

Someone in Congress, long ago, proposed that such people be allowed to "average" their incomes, so Farmer's tax would properly reflect a poor soul who earned just $10,425 taxable per year. After the dust had cleared from all the compromises, the legislated version of an "average" stretches a rather fundamental mathematical concept to new heights of distortion. The essence is that, in 1983, Farmer was taxed as though he had earned about $10,550 annually, a little bit more than the true average.

You have already done the bulk of the program to calculate a tax with income averaging, if you can accept ignoring such esoteric matters as certain income in certain community property states, premature IRA distributions, and foreign income. To come up with a 1983 version, a few more lines need to be added to the tax calculator used for Sally Single. With that program in your computer, type in these lines to increase the program's power:

PROGRAM 4D
Pre-1984 Income-averaging Calculator

```
650 GOSUB 13000
13000 R=T
13050 P=0
13100 PRINT "ENTER LAST 4 YEARS' INCOME:"
13150 FOR M=1 TO 4
13200 INPUT T
13210 PRINT T
```

```
13250 P=P+T
13300 NEXT M
13350 P=1.2*P/4
13400 G=I-P
13450 IF G<3000 THEN 14000
13500 G=(G*.2)+P
13550 I=P
13600 GOSUB 12050
13650 P=T
13700 I=G
13750 GOSUB 12050
13800 T=T+4*(T-P)
13850 PRINT "INC AVG TAX: $";T
13900 PRINT "REAL BRACKET: ";B*100;"%"
13950 PRINT "SAVINGS = $";R-T
14000 RETURN
```

If Frank were not single, it would be necessary to delete the data statements used for Sally Single before entering data from a different tax-rate schedule. That's blessedly not necessary this time, but we'll need a bit more of the data out of that same schedule, to take advantage of the tax calculation that uses lower brackets:

PROGRAM 4E
Frank Farmer's Tax-schedule Data

```
10650 DATA 4400,121,.13
10700 DATA 8500,251,.15
10750 DATA 10800,866,.17
10800 DATA 12900,1257,.19
```

Try running the program now, using Frank Farmer's story. Using 1983 taxable income of $34,100, it will start off with the same tax tale that Sally Single had, but it will then ask for the taxable income of the prior four years. For Frank, use "4500" for each of those years. If income averaging applies, your computer will tell you the new (lower) tax, the amount of tax saved using this technique, and the revised real bracket.

As expected, Frank's tax using income averaging is quite a bit lower—just $5,009, representing a savings of $2,954. Note also that his real bracket is just 19%. This means that any additional income (within limits) that Frank earns that year will be taxed at only 19%, whereas Sally Single, as we have seen, has the honor of contributing 40% of additional income to the government. If you don't believe this, rerun the program, using $34,225 income. On the $100 increase in income, the regular tax was bumped to $8,003, a $40 increase, and the tax calculated with income averaging hopped to $5,028, $19 more than before.

It is important to note that this has consequences that can be quite significant. This bracket applies to reductions in income, as well as increases. Since Sally is barely above the 36% bracket, if she puts $2,000 into an IRA, we would predict that she would save $720 (36% of $2,000), whereas an IRA for Frank would save only $380 (19% of $2,000). If you run the actual numbers through the program, you'll find the computed savings from IRA contributions to be $721 and $375, respectively. Certainly close enough for planning.

Although the difference between the IRA savings for the two taxpayers is enough to buy a pretty good night out on the town, please don't jump to false conclusions. Remember that the savings Frank realized from income averaging are good for a week or two in Europe. The point is that IRAs are more valuable to Sally than to Frank. Period. Each should use the appropriate tax savings in determining whether to make that IRA contribution in the first place. Nothing more.

The income-averaging version of the real bracket should be treated particularly diligently. Sally's bracket is fairly stable and can be used for future planning fairly confidently. Frank's income is unstable; he's likely to wind up uncomfortably settled once again in the poverty range, unable to think of tax savings as he struggles to buy pinto beans on sale.

Although income averaging was designed to protect financial fluctuators like Frank, it often applies to people who are advancing in their careers. In a world of inflation, when tax tables are not indexed, cost-of-living raises give the illusion that everyone is advancing, so there has been a marked increase in the '70s and '80s in the number of people who use this device. As this book is being written, the law officially indicates that taxes will be indexed to inflation, but there is significant doubt that this will really last. If it doesn't, income averaging would seem to continue to be a useful tax-saver for those who earn a "steady" income. Because this was apparent even on Capitol Hill, though, some of the spark was extinguished with the 1984 Tax Reform Act, as you will soon see.

The illusion of increasing income within the tax structure is the "bracket creep" referred to in the beginning of the chapter. Imagine that 1983 tax-rate schedules remain in effect for the next ten years, but that inflation erodes the value of a dollar to just a quarter. If your unmarried secretary earns $12,000 today and $48,000 in the inflated future, she really hasn't received a penny's worth of raise. But the tax table would show that she moved from the 19% tax bracket up to the 40% bracket. The first $100 cost-of-living raise added $19 to the tax bill; the last $100 raise added $40 to the tab. The only consolation for this bracket creep has been that income averaging might afford some partial relief.

This brings up another common myth. Income averaging can be used every year of your life, if you qualify, and if it's to your benefit. The authors have often become heroes simply by pointing this out to a lamenting soul with rising income who had used income averaging the previous year and was anxious to know when it could again be tried. The time is now.

Qualifying for income averaging is quite easy if you've been self-supporting and a U.S. resident during the "base" years. (Through 1983, the "base" years were the four years that preceded the year in question.) The main hurdle is that your current taxable income must be at least $3,000 more than the adjusted average of the income of those prior years. Recall that we indicated that the mathematical concept of "average" was distorted. To be more precise, the distortion has been that income of previous years was multiplied by 1.2. This adjusted average is calculated in line 13350 of Program 4D, and line 13450 performs the test for qualification. If averaging is not applicable, the other calculations are skipped, and the computer won't print out any results.

Income Averaging in Modern Times

That distortion factor was increased from 1.2 to 1.4 by the Tax Reform Act of 1984. This effectively raises the prior years' income in the calculation. The law also reduced the number of "base years" in the calculation from four to three. Because, in a world of inflation, the income of five years ago would tend to be the lowest, and thus the most beneficial, this will also tend to raise the "base-year" income. As you would expect, the higher the calculated prior years' income, the less benefit is to be gleaned from income averaging. Because the current year's high income now accounts for one-fourth of the period being averaged, instead of the one-fifth that many of us had grown to know and love, matters become even worse.

You can derive some degree of consolation from knowing that averaging has not been entirely eliminated and that you still have a useful program. To make the necessary changes, you need only enter (and save) the lines in Program 4F. Be sure the 1983 version is loaded before typing in the modifications.

PROGRAM 4F

1984 Income-averaging Modification

```
13100 PRINT "ENTER LAST 3 YEARS INCOME:"
13150 FOR M=1 TO 3
13350 P=1.4*P/3
13500 G=(G*.25)+P
13800 T=T+3*(T—P)
```

If you make this change, you may want to see what effect it has on Frank's tax picture. Using the same responses to each of the questions, with the exception that you will be allowed to enter only three years of prior income, you will find that the 1984 rules increased his liability by $306, to $5,315. As obnoxious as this is, though, it's only a glimpse of the real effect of these changes.

The increase in the distortion factor affects income of prior years. Because Frank's income in the preceding years was so miniscule, there just wasn't much to distort. Higher "base-year" incomes show more profound results. We entered data statements for the full 1983 Tax Rate Schedule X and looked at what happened to Helen Hotshot. Her earnings increased regularly; taxable income was $0 in 1979, $15,000 in 1980, $30,000 in 1981, $45,000 in 1982, and a whopping $80,000 in 1983. In 1983, income averaging was worth $4,584 in taxes saved; that's over 15% of her "regular" tax. If the 1984 law had been in effect then, however, she would have saved only $1,235. Her real tax bracket would have jumped from 40% to 45%. The infamous bottom line is that she would have made a contribution to the treasury of an additional $3,349. This illustrates one way in which the government can raise taxes without even touching the tax brackets.

When using the real bracket indicated by this program, it cannot be overemphasized that care must be employed. As was shown, the difference in bracket can be significant. Using income averaging one year does not imply eligibility in the following year, so the real bracket may be higher than you think. And *it is the expected real bracket that must be used to determine the tax consequences of investment decisions.* Last year's bracket is useful knowledge only to the degree that it can predict next year's. If income has jumped this year, do a quick income-averaging analysis to find out what bracket you are in this year.

To do this, you will have to insert the appropriate data statements from the tax-rate schedules. It's virtually impossible to determine which lines will apply. The only sure part of the bet is that you won't have to type in data statements for lines beyond those for the regular tax calculation. To be sure the program doesn't give wrong results, you should generally use *all* statements for brackets below those you would enter for the normal calculation. It may take a few minutes of typing, but it's a lot quicker and easier than muddling through the IRS forms. And it could keep you from making a costly error.

Before leaving the droll world of tax brackets to begin looking at more pleasant ways to invest your funds, a couple of additional cautions are in order. You may have noticed that neither Single nor Farmer paid state or local income taxes. This was by design, because these local taxes can cloud the bracket situation somewhat. The problem is that you can't simply add the effective state bracket to the federal, because the local taxes can be included among itemized deductions. This means that the higher your state bracket is, the greater the positive effect of the federal tax deduction. To complicate things even further, the laws governing what is taxable or deductible are often different from state taxes.

Most Americans are privileged with paying annual dues to their state capital as well as to Washington. As a general rule of thumb, if you multiply your real bracket by about 1.1, you'll have a better idea of your combined state and federal tax rate. Of course, like all rules of thumb, this can lead you down a garden path and into a briar patch. Nevertheless, it's somewhat better than totally ignoring the local responsibilities.

Deducting Your Computer

We also promised you a quick look at the effect of the 1984 Tax Reform Act with regard to deducting your computer. You may have heard that the new law has curtailed these tax benefits (among a number of others) for property used partially for business. The new rules may be somewhat nasty for you if you plugged in your computer, or a peripheral, for the first time after June 18, 1984. Such property must be depreciated using the "straight-line" method over twelve years *if* it is not used more than 50% for business purposes. The effect of this is to spread the allowable deductions over an interminably long period. Adding a bit more injury, if you have to use this slow, protracted depreciation, you are also ineligible to claim "investment credit" on the deductible portion. We'll discuss this credit a bit more in Chapter 9; for now, just realize that it's a juicy tax benefit, when you can get it.

Is the investment-related use discussed earlier considered "business" for purposes of the new law? Of course not; that would be too pleasant. Such use is deductible through depreciation, but only under the less beneficial twelve-year period, and investment credit disappears. The business use referred to here is your own trade or business. As an employee, to fulfill the "business" requirement, the use of the computer must be for the company's convenience *and* as a condition of employment; putting in time at home on weekends with a spreadsheet to impress the boss doesn't meet the test.

On a $90 computer that you've bought at the supermarket, the tax disadvantages aren't worth worrying about. But what if you bought a $6,000 Whiz-Bang PC System on June 19, 1984, for use exclusively in your self-employment and in your investments? We'll assume you're in a 40% tax bracket. If you use the computer *exactly* 50% for your business and 50% for your investments, you fail the test. In your first proud year of ownership, you'll be able to deduct a not-so-whopping $250, yielding $100 in tax savings. Your second year would be worth a $500 deduction, giving you $200 in benefits. It is presumed that you will stop using the machine for anything other than an overgrown paperweight long before the 12-year period has expired.

But what if you use the computer 50.1% of the time for business and 49.9% for investments? Or if you plugged it in one day earlier? You can take investment credit, worth an immediate $600 in tax benefits. You can deduct depreciation of $855, yielding $342 in tax savings. The second year is worth $1,254 in deductions and $502 in tax benefits. Add up the figures; the total *difference* in tax benefits as a result of passing the "business-use" test is $1,144 in the first two years. In a bureaucratic jungle, something as seemingly insignificant as a fraction of a percent in use can have a profound effect on the bottom line. To make matters worse, the 50-50 arrangement will never recoup the $600 investment-credit advantage.

Another provision in the new law has a bearing on *everyone* who deducts a portion of their personal computers, regardless of the time of purchase. Beginning in 1985, "adequate contemporaneous records" must be kept to substantiate deductibility. We're confident that the IRS and the court will be expending a fair amount of time, effort, and tax dollars in the coming years determining exactly what is and what isn't "adequate." But, if the potential benefits of deductions are worth the effort, you probably should get into the habit of keeping some sort of log of computer time devoted to various activities.

Don't expect a lot of friendly after-the-fact help from your neighborhood tax preparer if you fail to keep records. He or she will be required to obtain a written statement from you saying that they really exist. Failure to do this could subject the poor preparer to penalties. And you'll probably be charged for any time you spend arguing the point.

Actually, there is a bright side to this: it could have been worse. The Senate originally wanted the preparer to actually verify the records. This could have allowed you the honor of paying the accountant to perform a mini-audit of your claimed deductions.

All of this shows a clear trend. Washington seems determined to put tax preparers in the awkward position of examining your data for the IRS, while you pay for the job. Believe it or not, the American Institute of CPAs, to their credit, argued against this, resulting in the compromise that we are now required to endure. It is probably nonetheless only a matter of time before your favorite accountant no longer knows whose side he's on, even though he is fully aware of who pays the bills.

On to Happier Thoughts

The more your tax advisors become constrained, the more important it will become for you to be able to fend for yourself in the jungle of the Internal Revenue Code. The several groups of statements you've entered have become a powerful tax tool that can be used in inexpensive computers. It will often be necessary to know your real tax bracket when using other programs in the book. Use last year's tax return as a starting point in figuring this year's taxable income. Then look up your bracket; last year's schedules will give you a good approximation. If you think income averaging may apply to you, all you need to do is put in the necessary data statements to handle your situation. But first delete the statements you entered to run the examples. Deleting these is, perhaps, the simplest "program" you will ever enter:

    10650
    10700
    10750
    10800
    11050
    11100
    11150

If only your taxes could disappear that easily!

5
Money Markets

This chapter is a good place to start some serious programming, because it proceeds on considerations of money alone. Whereas the stock market may be a test of skill or luck, and the real estate market may be a test of judgment or endurance, the money market is a test only of computation. There will be occasions in this chapter when we will make reference to somewhat riskier themes, such as currency speculation or investments that are not strictly time deposits, such as municipal bond funds, but these are presented for edification rather than computation.

How much advice do you imagine that people could need on something as simple as savings accounts? Plenty, apparently. As April 15 approaches, a television ad featuring a folksy cowboy actor is featured many times per night, advertising IRAs at a large savings and loan in the western U.S. These bankers, the ad claims, are so eager to serve you they will be staying open until nine every night for two weeks. What's more, the cowboy beams, those fellers will even let you *charge your IRA deposit to your VISA or Mastercharge!* Now we doubt they would put that in the ad if some people didn't do it. Let us examine this offer for a moment.

This institution will let you borrow their money, and will charge you 21% interest, if you give it right back to them in an account that pays 9%. Do you see what's wrong with that deal?!

If you are expecting a windfall in the next month and will pay back the credit card right away, that would be an acceptable use of this dodge. If you are thinking of paying back the credit card gradually, it is much less acceptable. Actually, this scenario approaches a kind of surrealistic banker's heaven, in which people who don't even need the money take out loans for the privilege of paying an interest differential. The only thing that makes this remotely plausible is the way that taxation affects this deal—in some circumstances it can look all right on paper, but with an important catch that we will examine later in this chapter.

There are, in our experience, a great many persons who have what they think are savings, financed by borrowing. If you are one of these persons, please consider the following perspective on your situation: if you owe money on consumer loans or credit cards to a bank, then a) your actual net savings is your savings minus this debt, and b) if the debt exceeds your savings, you are making, effectively, negative interest on the savings. If you have an 18% consumer loan for $1,000 and a 5% passbook account with $1,000 in it, you are paying $(18\% - 5\%) * 100 = \$130$ per year for the privilege of pretending to yourself that you have some savings. This is not how people get ahead financially.

But it is how many otherwise intelligent people behave; there is something about compound interest that seems to fog the minds of normally clear-headed individuals. If you are beyond this type of elementary error of judgment (or have somehow landed in the 50% bracket, in which Wonderland economics works out in some cases), some of the material in this chapter may seem quite obvious. Curiously though, it appears that it is nonetheless almost desperately necessary.

Into the Computer

The first point to observe is that you will invariably be asked to enter an interest rate in every program. In retrospect, one of the most remarkable features of post–World War II economic history in the United States is how stable interest rates were for so long; the surprise is not that they jump around so much now but that they were so inert through much of the 1950s and 1960s. One model for this situation might be to regard all other national economies in the 1950s as essentially collapsed because of the war, turning the United States into the only serious manufacturing economy in a universe of passive suppliers of abundant raw materials. As cannot have escaped your attention, this is not what is happening in 1985 and beyond. The American economy, because of its relative political stability, is attractive to foreign capital, and the interest rates here jump around a great deal with fluctuation in the demand for dollars, both external and internal (government deficit financing being a particularly controversial factor in rate determination). Thus, all calculations in this chapter start with an interest rate, which presumably you will get from your morning newspaper. It will generally also be a good idea to pay attention to the balance of speculation on interest-rate changes in the next six months to one year.

The Basics

We will start here fairly slowly, so slowly, in fact, that we will not actually produce a program just yet but will beat a few elementary points to death by way of warm-up exercise.

In the financial pages of a California newspaper this morning several banks (this term will cover savings and loans as well) are bidding for your attention with fabulous rates for your IRA deposit. Please note that they are much more interested in an IRA account than in the flighty one-year deposit of days gone by—nothin' like that good ole long-term money. Expressed in terms of annual yield, a concept whose explanation will be included in the program to follow, the offers are:

XYZ Savings 11.23%
Global Savings 11.56%
Wafflington Bank 11.33%

With these annual yields, your return on $2,000 is going to be (do this on a calculator, or, for that matter, in your head):

XYZ Savings $224.60
Global Savings $231.20
Wafflington Bank $226.60

As you look down in stunned outrage at the book in your hands, wondering how anyone could have the effrontery to point out anything so simple, we hasten to make our point before you hurl this volume at your cat. The point is, the difference in yield on these accounts for a whole year would not pay for parking all afternoon in most major-city downtown areas. If you already bank at Wafflington because you like the cute pictures of horses on the checkbooks, it is definitely not worth making a separate trip across town to Global, much less XYZ. The situation here is that for the same type of account, virtually all institutions will pay virtually the same rate. You really needn't shop around much. The point at which things may get confusing is when an institution attempts to mask a somewhat lower rate by quoting simple interest on a time deposit of several years. First, let's type in a starting-point program, and then we'll see how this works.

PROGRAM 5A
Elements of Interest

```
100 PRINT "RATE=?"
150 INPUT R
200 PRINT R
250 PRINT "TIMEBASE=?"
300 INPUT T
350 PRINT "YRS=?"
400 INPUT N
450 LET Z=N*T
500 LET N=R/(100*T)
550 LET B=2000*(1+N) ↑ Z
600 PRINT "BAL=$";B
```

Once this program is typed in, save it. You may wish to call it something evocative like "5A" when you save it; given that you have bought this book, you can look up remarks about the program content easily enough here.

This straightforward effort, which is simple enough to have been included in another form in *Basic Money*, at least has the advantage of explaining why most savings accounts quote two figures for you, the current annual rate and the current annual yield. Please note, as a noncomputational matter, the stress on the word "current." It is an alarmingly common practice for banks and others to quote a tremendous "current" rate on IRA accounts, in particular in March, to attract customers. In the fine print it will usually say somewhere that the rate on the account will sink like a stone on April 15. You must check to see whether the rate is variable and how it is determined (many accounts are regulated by the current interest on Treasury bills).

Run this program for the inputs RATE=11, TIMEBASE=1, and YRS=1. This is a computation of simple interest for 11% for one year, and because of our constant reference to $2,000, this is the assumed deposit. TIMEBASE=1 means that the compounding period is just once per year. The output from this not exactly earthshaking effort should be:

```
RATE=?
11
TIMEBASE=?
YRS=?
BAL=$ 2220
```

This just says, of course, that 11% simple interest on $2,000 gives you $2,220 at the end of the year, not surprising as $220 is 11% of $2,000. Now run this again, and when the TIMEBASE prompt comes up input 365 instead—this corresponds to interest being compounded daily (that is, the time base is one day). Now for a balance you should get:

```
BAL=$2232.52
```

so that, just as you would expect, you make more money if your savings are compounded daily. We will want to put in a little extension of the program to calculate the new rate, so at this point call up the "saved" program called 5A and add this to it:

```
550 LET X=(1+ N)↑Z
600 PRINT "BAL=$"; 2000*X
650 PRINT "YIELD="; (1−X)*100
```

When you run this program it will take the simple interest you input, usually the "current annual rate" in a newspaper ad, and at the end of the program give back a "current annual yield." Note that a little of the arithmetic has been shifted into the PRINT lines. All that is going on in line 650 is that the interest factor X is being converted to a rate in the same format as the rate you used for input (that is, 12 as a rate means 12%, so you don't have to put in 0.12 instead).

One of the things you may discover as you poke through newspaper ads with this program is that many banks treat IRA accounts differently from passbook savings or certificates of deposit with respect to compounding. Because you may withdraw your money from the other accounts on a more regular basis, the interest is almost invariably compounded daily. In an IRA, some institutions compound quarterly and some just credit simple interest at the end of the year, principally because they feel that once they have your money they don't have to compete over fractions of a percent (the "premature distribution" penalties are sufficiently discouraging).

Because the subject of arithmetic has raised its tiresome head, we may as well point out that different computers have slightly different levels of accuracy in number storage and rounding off. Some versions of Microsoft BASIC apparently give $2,232.47 instead of $2,232.52 as the balance in the example above; the extra nickel is presumably lost somewhere in the computer. Usually this is not a problem; the programs here, in most cases, are supposed to illustrate points and compare alternatives, and this can be done with great clarity even if your computer loses a few pennies in multiplying from time to time.

With the addition and alteration of the few lines noted, please save the changed program as 5AX (for "extended 5A"). You can make up your own name if you wish, but 5AX will be the reference name in this book. Anyway, try these examples, taken directly from the pages of a newspaper:

  a. Use RATE=12.5, TIMEBASE=365,YRS=1
     (You should get a balance of $2,266.25 and a yield of 13.31.)
  b. Use RATE=9.8, TIMEBASE=365,YRS=1
     (You should get a balance of $2,205.90 and a yield of 10.29.)

One other modification you might like to try assumes that everyone will be compounding daily (although this is not always the case) and requires the addition of these lines:

```
250 LET T=365
300
```

The second statement just serves to erase the old line 300; when you LIST the program there will be no line 300 there. With this program, let's poke around to determine the meaning of a newspaper ad that claims to give "35% yield on a five-year CD." The CD, in case you are new to these matters, stands for certificate of deposit; it effectively locks up your money, in this case for five years. What the statement above really means is that at the end of five years the yield on your deposit, here taken as $2,000, will have been 35%. What is the annual rate to compare to this?

You must in this case experiment a little, trying out different RATEs and keeping YRS at 5. What emerges is that the annual rate is 6%, for an annual yield of 6.18%. Although 35% seems like a lot of interest, the catch is that over five years it gives just the modest rate of 6% as an annual figure and was thus the worst deal in the paper on the day in question. Keep your eye on the "current annual yield," which is usually mentioned somewhere; this is the easiest figure to use to determine what you are really being offered.

This program and a little common sense are all that you will need to make distinctions among time deposits. The common sense is required because you must make, in ordinary accounts and time deposits, a decision about deposit term. Is it worth tying up your savings for three years at a 10% fixed rate, or would you be better off going for a ninety-day deposit at 9.25%, figuring that the rates would be above 11% later in the year? In general, the longer-time deposits carry higher fixed rates, but you may find that the difference, compared to shorter terms, is not great enough to make you want to lock up your money for longer than six months or a year. This is the kind of exciting decision that is part of household finance in the late 1980s, and unfortunately there is no convincing way to program a conclusion about future interest rates.

An IRA: What If You Want Your Money Back?

All this business about time deposits is well and good if you have sacks of currency lying around and can postpone any bad luck until you are sixty. There is no doubt about it, if you have $2,000 that you will not need over the next thirty years, the only intelligent move is to put it in an IRA. In a well-ordered household in which budgets are worked out to 2% accuracy and nothing ever happens unexpectedly, this is how old folks get to take Caribbean cruises.

What happens if you have a sudden and drastic need for some money, but have all your savings locked up in an IRA?

This fretful topic is something that the savings institutions are not especially eager to discuss, but it is also something that happens to real people in real life, so the subject is fair game for a program.

The financial advisors in every magazine and newspaper column tell you never to touch your IRA. Upon approaching the new-accounts desk of various institutions the authors have found that the cheerful and eager smile of the typical new-accounts person turns to a look of frozen hostility when "premature distribution" (that's early withdrawal from an IRA) is mentioned. The result of this is that frequently people end up borrowing money rather than touching their own savings to pay unanticipated debts. Property-tax increases or income-tax miscalculations frequently appear in this connection. On a more pragmatic note, you could also be forgiven for wondering if an IRA is a good place to try to save up for a mortgage down payment. Will the penalties cancel out the benefits of compounding on all that untaxed money? This is an area in which intuitive estimates are usually wrong, which means that it is time for a program.

Use This Program Only in Emergency

Type Program 5B in, and after it has been run a few times to check for correctness, you will want to save it on tape or disk for a very rainy day indeed.

PROGRAM 5B
IRA Penalties

```
100  LET V=.35
125  PRINT "RATE ONE=?.MONTHS=?"
150  INPUT Q
175  INPUT L
200  PRINT"RATE TWO=?.MONTHS=?"
225  INPUT W
250  INPUT N
275  LET T=(1+Q/1200)↑L
300  LET S=(1+W/1200)↑N
325  LET B=2000*S*T
350  PRINT "BAL =$";B
```

```
375 PRINT "PENALTY=$";0.1*B
400 PRINT "TAX = $";B*V
425 PRINT "NET = $"; B*(0.9−V)
450 PRINT "NON-IRA RATE=?"
475 INPUT R
500 LET C=2000*(1−V)
525 LET C=C* (1+(1−V)*R/1200)↑(L+N)
550 PRINT "ALT.ACCT.=$";C
```

The program calls for two sets of rates and times. This is because the interest-penalty problem, which is different from the federal early-withdrawal penalty, is usually set out in an IRA account booklet as no interest (or a very low rate) for a certain number of months and then another rate (which may be the original rate or may be less) for the rest of the term. The other rate called for as an input is the interest rate for a non-IRA account at the same institution, for comparison. The program assumes a 35% marginal tax bracket in line 100; change this to your own bracket if you wish.

First we will look at a sample run for an early withdrawal and explain a little more about program assumptions. The penalties at Benign Savings are loss of three month's interest on accounts held for longer than a year. We will take the example of an account being closed out after four years. the run looks like this:

```
RATE ONE=?.MONTHS=?
? 0
? 3
RATE TWO=?.MONTHS=?
? 10
? 45
BAL=$ 2905.47
PENALTY=$ 290.547
TAX=$ 1016.91
NET=$ 1598.01
NON-IRA RATE=?
? 8
ALT.ACCT.=$1599.85
```

This means zero interest for three months, 10% for forty-five months, and 8% on non-IRA accounts. The amount assumed is $2,000, and compounding is done monthly as a compromise between the variety of schemes in practice. The alternate account starts with the deposit of $2,000 after taxes, in this case $1,300, and provides for income tax on the interest as it accumulates.

First you will see some bad news. After the interest penalty, the federally imposed 10% penalty for premature distribution, and ordinary income tax on the amount you take out, the amount in your account is cut practically in half. Note that different banks can mean slightly different things by the three-months'-interest penalty, but the method here is a reasonable approximation of typical practice.

Next, however, you see something that may be unexpected and should be considered mildly good news. Although your savings on paper are cut to pieces, you have ended up with nearly the same amount you would have collected from an ordinary time deposit account at a slightly lower rate. Remember that the money to open a non-IRA account would have been taxable right from the start, and that the interest on it is also taxed. This calculation is predicated upon Benign Savings' relatively kindly policy of enforcing the minimum interest penalty for early withdrawal. Not all institutions have the same penalties, and you *must* investigate these things carefully. Some banks take away practically all your interest; some CD accounts at brokerage houses let you keep nearly all of it. Unless you have a functioning crystal ball in good repair, this information is critical.

Whether or not you can outperform a non-IRA investment despite withdrawal penalties depends on the penalty policies of the institution and the amount of time the money can be deposited. The First Nasty Bank, where ironically both of the authors have accounts, has this schedule for early withdrawal: no interest on six months and 5.25% on the rest. When you try this case in the program, for our four-year example, you get:

```
RATE ONE=?.MONTHS=?
? 0
? 6
RATE TWO=?.MONTHS=?
? 5.25
? 42
BAL=$ 2402.45
```

```
PENALTY=$ 240.245
TAX=$ 840.859
NET=$ 1321.35
NON-IRA RATE=?
? 8
ALT.ACCT.=$1599.85
```

As you can see, the First Nasty Bank leaves you in pretty rough shape. The penalties even at four years are sufficient to make a non-IRA deposit a better idea. This information is useful in planning where you might like to keep your IRA account; if you ever think you might need the money back sooner than age fifty-nine and a half, you should be willing to trade a little in interest rate for a kindlier interest-penalty policy. And yet, we have been assured by countless officers in charge of new accounts, this is something that is seldom asked about when the account is opened.

For further enlightenment, and because we will need the data, consider these program runs: a two-year IRA at Benign Savings and thirteen months at First Nasty Bank, first, for two years at Benign Savings.

```
RATE ONE=?.MONTHS=?
? 0
? 3
RATE TWO=?.MONTHS=?
? 10
? 21
BAL=$ 2380.77
PENALTY=$ 238.077
TAX=$ 833.268
NET=$ 1309.42
NON-IRA RATE=?
? 8
ALT.ACCT.=$1442.15
```

Thirteen months at First Nasty produces these results:

```
RATE ONE=?.MONTHS=?
? 0
? 6
RATE TWO=?.MONTHS=?
? 5.25
? 7
```

```
BAL=$ 2062.06
PENALTY=$ 206.206
TAX=$ 721.72
NET=$ 1134.13
NON-IRA RATE=?
? 8
ALT.ACCT.=$1375.17
```

The moral of the story is, no matter how kindly the withdrawal policy, you will get clobbered if you need your money back anytime soon. On a deposit that can be left for four years or so, the compounding of the originally untaxed sum overcomes the penalties, but for shorter periods there is no hope.

Wonderland Revisited

Now we are in a position to return to the offer made by the genial cowboy at the beginning of this chapter. The tax laws have the effect, past a certain marginal bracket, of making ordinarily straightforward assumptions as unreliable as croquet played with hedgehogs for croquet balls—hence the section title. This will be useful for attitude adjustment also, because it will be clear that the Red Queen was largely responsible for most real-estate tax law to be presented later.

Say you borrow $2,000 on a credit card and pay it back in regular installments over five years, following a schedule that is just twice the minimum payment plan for a $1,000 debt. This will result in the payment of a little more than $1,000 in interest over the five years. You can take this figure on faith, or you can follow the explanation of credit card payments in *Basic Money*. This interest will be tax-deductible, resulting in some effective savings on taxes. Furthermore, because this $2,000 was put in an IRA, there are tax savings for the first year also. You begin paying interest on the credit-card debt but are earning tax-deferred interest, albeit at a much lower rate, in an IRA. So where does this leave you after five years?

This is a nearly perfect example of the need for a computer to do investment calculations. Even though the figures for net proceeds for an early-withdrawal IRA are approximate, they are a tremendous improvement on intuition. Table 5A summarizes the situation for three different brackets.

Table 5A Credit-Card IRA after Five Years

	Tax Bracket		
	20%	35%	45%
Tax saved in year one	$400	$700	$900
Pmts on card, adj for tax	$2800	$2650	$2550
Net pmt	$2400	$1950	$1650
IRA acct at 9%	$3131	$3131	$3131
Early withdraw at Benign	$2143	$1684	$1378
Early withdraw at Nasty	$1772	$1392	$1139

This curious chart will bear some examination. First, please note that the scheme more or less works at all income levels shown, *as long as you don't want your money back.* If you try to make a withdrawal from your IRA, you get back less money than you deposited. The premature distribution provisions of IRAs are designed to wipe out the tax advantages, and that's just what they do. Next, please note the incredible implicit encouragement that the law gives to persons in the 45% bracket to form an IRA. Although the money is pretty much locked in the account (look at the withdrawal penalty!) a mere $1,450 will buy $3,131 in (pre-tax) retirement funds. And that's on an IRA financed with a credit card. Obviously, they could do even better starting the account with cash.

An IRA may not really be worth as much in constant dollars as this type of calculation indicates. There are nagging problems with inflation and changes in taxation schemes that could make all this less favorable. At the moment, though, high-bracket families have little to lose; when you would just be sending the money to the IRS anyway, putting a few thousand in an IRA is certainly a harmless move. If the effective yield gets eaten by inflation, it's just a partial loss of money that was going to be confiscated anyway.

By the way, if you read this far you may as well be told that various advanced thinkers have proposed that Social Security benefits be adjusted according to the size of your IRA balance upon retirement: large balance means smaller benefits. This would be a first step in converting Social Security from a government-backed pension plan to a form of welfare; that is, if you have a reasonable retirement account the government figures you are on your own. It will be interesting to see how this and related proposals fare in the strange decades ahead.

Good News for the Gutless

Even a fairly timid soul can sleep safely at night thinking of his or her money in an IRA. Although the deposits certainly aren't very liquid, as long as the interest rate is higher than the inflation rate, the money is at least earning something. There are two more financial instruments that operate at about the same level of safety and that also earn tax-free interest. If you dislike the whiff of gambling that rises from even the tamest stock-market play, and if you don't want to be someone's landlord, these are worth looking into; for some reason they have exceptionally good yields at the moment (mid-1980s).

The two investments to be discussed are municipal bonds and annuities. Let us state at the outset that you may as well skip this section if you don't have enough surplus funds to make the maximum contribution to an IRA. The yields on these investments are tax-free, of course, but will generally be lower than the yield in an IRA. Typically, it is easier to get your money back out of these investments than from an IRA, but that's because you deposit money in them that has already been taxed. The other point to make about these investments is that, as you will see shortly, you have to be in a high marginal bracket for them to be really attractive.

Program 5C is a simple program to determine the effective yield on a tax-free investment. After running a few examples of this, we will also consider some of the market aspects of municipal bonds and annuities; they are not invariably as sure a thing as an insured certificate of deposit in a bank.

PROGRAM 5C
Tax-deferred Yield

```
 50 PRINT "FED BRACKET"
100 INPUT F
150 PRINT F
200 PRINT "STATE BRACKET"
```

```
250 INPUT S
300 PRINT S
350 D=(F + ((100—F)*S/100)/100
400 V=1/(1—D)
450 PRINT "COMB.BRKT(%)="; D*100
500 PRINT "TAX-FREE YIELD =?"
550 INPUT Y
600 PRINT Y
650 V=Y*V
700 PRINT "EQUIV YIELD = ";Y
```

This program is certainly straightforward, but it has its uses; the calculation is used frequently in advertising for tax-free bond funds, proclaiming equivalent yields of 16% or so when the regular interest rate is 10%. Try these numbers: federal tax bracket—32%, state bracket—6%, and investment yield—8.7%. For this situation, which does not by any means imply tremendous income, the equivalent yield is 13.6%. That's a very nice yield. So what's the problem, you may ask, and why doesn't everyone get in on this act? As an answer, we provide a brief review of what can go wrong.

Annuities You must first find out three things: a) what the sales charge is (in some cases it is zero), b) what the withdrawal penalties are (these also may be zero after five to ten years, an advantage over IRAs), and c) what the administrative fees are each year (these cut into your interest). You should also look into the rate that the annuity fund has paid over the last five to ten years, to check that it tracks the interest rate reasonably well. Some funds are based on stock portfolios that do very well and some are based on portfolios that go either nowhere or, heaven forfend, down. Different insurance companies offer annuities in different styles. A standard deal is to make the lump deposit of five to ten thousand dollars, let this accumulate the tax-deferred interest over many years, and then dole out the proceeds as monthly payments. Another deal consists of building up the deposit with monthly payments; this could be useful to you if you need to be nagged to save. In either case, it is usually possible to take the funds from a mature annuity and deposit them where they will give the best return. Thus, if you don't mind talking to lots of people from insurance companies, you may find an annuity that is a desirable place to park non-IRA funds while you age gracefully.

Municipal bonds The most convenient way to get into the municipal bond market is through bond funds typically assembled by brokerage firms; these allow participation with as little as $500 in some cases. The "catch" in this arrangement is that if interest rates rise, the underlying value of shares in the bond fund drops. That means that if you want your money back right away you will suffer a loss on your capital. Suppose you buy $1,000 worth of a fund that is paying a tax-free 8% when you start. If the interest rate on regular taxable deposits rises from 13% to 15% over the year, you would likely find that, although you get to keep your $80 in interest, the thousand dollars would now be worth something like $870. This is simply a feature of bonds—they promise a certain payment, and the value of the bond adjusts itself so that this payment will correspond to the prevailing interest rate. Tax-free bonds always pay lower interest than corporate bonds, but at times the difference becomes amazingly small, given the advantages of tax exemption. What you need to do (and again, this is probably to be done with surplus savings beyond your IRA contribution) is to shop around for a fund with the smallest possible fees and service charges, and then decide if the credit markets are likely to be stable for some time.

If you are interested, here is a program fragment to tack onto the end of Program 5C:

```
750  PRINT "RATE CHANGE =?"
800  INPUT D
850  PRINT D
900  N=10*Y/V−D*V*700/Y
950  PRINT "NET = ";N
```

It assumes a $1,000 investment and a ratio of 0.7 for the interest paid on a tax-free bond compared to a taxable-yield bond; this ratio is historically fairly correct. The output from this section is your net gain or loss on a one-year deal in which you close out the bond position after collecting one year's interest. The input called for is the difference in corporate bond rates (just take a T-bill rate, if you are lazy) for the beginning and end of the year—+2 would mean the rates went up 2%, and −4, correspondingly, means a four-point drop. This is approximate, because your loss, up to a point, is tax-deductible, but the program is worth trying a few times. It will show, among other things, that this type of market is proabably more suited to people who can leave their money for a long time and thus not worry too much about bond price fluctuation.

Bon Voyage

For the adventurous, there is one last side-avenue in the world of money that we should mention, namely, currency speculation. As this is written (mid-1980s), the dollar is considered to be painfully overvalued compared to the currencies of several other nations, most notably Japan. Because Japan is a country almost entirely dependent on exporting manufactured goods, the Japanese government puts a considerable effort into making yen cheap compared to dollars. In the U.S., firms that rely on exporting would in turn prefer to see a cheaper dollar. This tug-of-war, with other struggles in British pounds, German marks, and Swiss francs, is likely to continue, with attendant shifts in exchange rates over the years.

If you are willing to devote a reasonable amount of time to studying the market in foreign exchange, you can often see shifts coming months in advance. If you are ridiculously prosperous or foolhardy, you can trade currency futures options. This has the risks implicit in all types of margin trading (see stern warnings in earlier chapters). You can, however, if you shop around, find traveler's checks issued specifically by foreign-currency traders that have virtually no service charges. If you buy yen-denominated traveler's checks and hold them during a 5% upward adjustment of the yen against the dollar, you would get to keep nearly the whole 5%; this sort of move can take place in a few weeks or a month, and thus provides a return better than any standard deposit, without a large risk (this is not a margin trade, and for that matter the checks are insured).

Although this is not the sort of thing you would want to count on for retirement, it is an area in which larger trends are often fairly clear; a close reading of the currency market section of the *Economist* has proved to be sufficient for calling most major changes. Even if you never start trading in foreign exchange, it is worth looking into these matters to sharpen your understanding of the external influences on the interest rates paid on dollar accounts in the U.S.

6
Stocks, Bonds, and Options

The attractions of the stock market as an investment are many, but perhaps even more numerous are its attractions as a pastime. For much less than the price of a decent sailboat, for example, you have an activity rich in social possibilities; you can chat with a broker and other investors, you can hang around brokerage offices and watch the stock trades roll by on a large screen; you can get the newspaper, preferably the *Wall Street Journal,* and leave it around at work with the stock pages marked up as a way of striking up conversations. For less than the price of a set of golf clubs or tennis lessons you can enjoy these same benefits in the now-booming options market (for those who pay no attention to these things, in the so-called index options you can bet a few hundred at a time simply on the market direction, up or down).

It is by no means clear, given the investment performance of the typical smaller investor (or a great many larger ones, for that matter), that these noneconomic features of the market are not subtly more important than the profit motive. You can feel economically sophisticated if you know something about the market, and above all it gives you something to do. After all, the point of having money itself is ultimately to give you something to do, and following the market gives you something to do whether you are making money or not. It rather effectively disguises the motives that lure people across the desert to Las Vegas behind the appearance of rock-solid upper-middle-class respectability. A gambler drives a pink Cadillac convertible with fins and gold-plated bumpers; you, as a serious investor, drive a dark blue Mercedes diesel. At least, that's the outward image, despite the sporting instincts lurking in both of you.

This book, however, is really being written for the kind of dreary characters who want to earn somewhat better returns on their money than ordinary passbook interest. It has grown out of the authors' observations about their own struggles, and those of others around them, to perform simple economic functions such as buying a house, raising a family, and saving a little for retirement. These functions were somewhat more straightforward in the earlier world of 4% home loans to GIs and 2% inflation. If you are between the ages of twenty-five and forty, ask yourself how much effort you will have to put into buying a house comparable to the one you lived in when you were ten. Half of the conversations in up-scale bars in San Francisco, New York, and Washington, D.C., are the sound of young professionals speculating on the finagling they will have to do to get themselves a modest house of the type that a factory worker could have bought without thinking twice in the 1950s.

Nonetheless, there is hope. It happens that some investment strategies are demonstrably better than others. The one that will evolve in this chapter, although fairly boring, can be shown to work fairly well. In fact *you* can show that it works fairly well, on your own computer, before you have to bet real money on it. If you would like more excitement in your life, we can recommend this composite strategy: a) follow the sober course outlined here in the market, and b) take up hang-gliding and take out an enormous life-insurance policy (a term policy, not whole life, but more on that later) at the same time.

Ups and Downs

Rather than say that stock prices are purely random, or that on the other hand their value is determined by fundamental business considerations, we will state at the outset a few compromises. We believe that a certain percentage of the price of a stock reflects the value of a company and its expected earnings. Another percentage of the price represents simply the result of random sales and purchases of the stock by independent investors (by independent we mean only that they are not in collusion with one another). The judgment of the relative importance of these two factors is, of course, what this business is all about. We contend that an examination of some fundamental considerations, most of which are simply the necessary mathematics of the statistical consequences of large numbers of independent actions, will lead to some predictions for stock-market strategy that are testable, and particularly testable on a small computer.

Program 6A performs the simplest kind of random walk. Just type it in, and then we'll explain the assumptions and tell you a little bit about random walks.

PROGRAM 6A
Random Stock-walk

```
100 LET B=40
150 RANDOMIZE
200 LET V=3
250 FOR K=1 TO 20
300 LET A=RND
350 IF A<=.5 THEN T=−1
400 IF A>.5 THEN T=1
450 LET P=RND
500 LET B=B+T*V*P
550 PRINT B
600 NEXT K
650 INPUT "CONTINUE? Y=1, N=0"
675 INPUT D
700 IF D=1 THEN GOTO 250
750 END
```

Here's what is happening in this program. We start with an arbitrary stock price of $40 (B=40). Then we call the computer's random-number generator to start; it will either "initialize" itself automatically or ask you for a seed number that you pick out (−31, +5, −5555, or whatever you like); it then sets up a string of random numbers between 0 and 1. The first number is used to pick a step direction, up or down; if this first number is less than one-half we step down, and if it is greater than one-half we step up. The next random number gives us the amount of the step. Here we are allowing a maximum step size of $3. Thus, on any given day, our stock can go up $3, go down $3, or do anything in between. We have

set the FOR . . . NEXT loop size to 20, just to give the equivalent
of four weeks of market action for a single run (and also so
that the display will fit on your screen). At the end of the program is a little decision flag—you can continue the same run
or get out and start a new one.

Note that if you have a really eccentric computer you will
have to look at the manual for a little advice about how to
get the random-number generator started. If it's not initialized
properly you get the same string of random numbers every
time (maybe this is what happens every day in the special
part of hell reserved for stock brokers . . . they have to watch
an identical set of random numbers parade by on the ticker).
The $3 step size may seem arbitrary, but it really isn't; we
picked it after measuring about two weeks' worth of jumps
in the stock pages. Here are some sample runs for discussion:

40.8005	40.2102	37.6735	37.056
39.4051	41.7414	39.7021	38.4557
39.0893	44.0909	37.2142	36.7963
39.775	44.2792	35.7921	37.812
41.3825	41.517	37.4672	36.2257
40.1564	43.1307	34.6117	36.5286
38.0152	43.0126	36.7764	39.0651
37.2196	43.9019	37.5928	40.2027
37.409	44.3581	36.1757	40.0956
37.7465	45.3996	37.1338	39.2814
37.7743	42.6785	39.4011	37.5073
38.5929	44.6257	39.0408	35.1262
36.1414	42.3723	40.72	32.295
37.9085	41.8514	42.0576	30.0048
37.5578	44.7523	43.3765	30.4523
37.2101	42.1076	41.0082	32.23
36.7097	40.3846	38.7541	31.5024
37.3891	41.2108	40.2313	31.9527
36.0593	40.9858	40.6347	33.3466
34.089	38.5519	42.4417	35.4385

We are not plotting this material because we want to make
this work on all sorts of computers, some with odd, small displays as well. If you have the patience to get out a piece of
graph paper and plot a good run, you will make the ominous

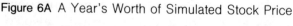

Figure 6A A Year's Worth of Simulated Stock Price

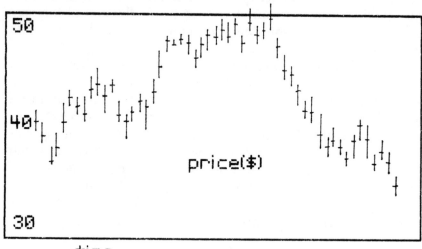

observation that *it looks just like a real stock!* This is the program that generated the examples of real stock vs. simulation in Chapter 2.

It is characteristic of a random walk that, if you wait long enough, it should pass at some time through every possible numerical value. "Long enough" in this case could mean a very long time indeed, but nonetheless you are assured, for example, that the little program written above will run from a starting point of 40 into negative (that is, meaningless) values. We will take up this point in a second, but first let us take a look at a random run of 52 points, corresponding to the way stock prices are represented for a year in books compiled by charting services (see Figure 6A).

This program will typically start giving suspiciously unrealistic values only for runs of several hundred steps, and even then everything will usually look all right. But right now, with Figure 6A before our eyes, there are some crucial points to observe, points that we will need later in this chapter when we formulate a strategy for stock selection:

Point one In the short run, the price of a stock can look just like a random walk. The price appears to have no "memory" of its direction.

Point two In the long run, the price *can't* be random, because stocks do not wander off into negative prices unless something weird indeed has happened.

These points added together will suggest a plan that has a reasonably sound mathematical basis and some practical economic underpinnings as well. For the moment we will draw only the lesson that it is difficult to forecast the short-term price movement of a stock, and we will see what practical advice we can derive from such a simple statement.

Knockout in the First Round

There is little justification for inserting in such a sober work as the one before you a jeremiad on the dangers of commodities trading. If your mother didn't warn you against soybean futures as well as against friends who drink too much, she was simply remiss in her maternal duties. And if that didn't scare you, the size of the balance that a reputable firm will want you to leave in your account if you start doing futures trading should make you wonder if this represents a prudent pastime. In a country, however, in which a great many people spend Monday morning rehashing the egregious blunders made by well-paid football players on the preceding day, perhaps it is not surprising that there are tens of thousands of people who think they can call the wheat market better than the Cargill organization in Minneapolis.

The point to be made here is not that you can't call the wheat market better than Cargill or Continental Grain; maybe you can. At issue is the purely mathematical circumstance that you are quite likely to be blown out of the water before you get a chance to prove yourself right. In the interests of education, please call up Program 6A from tape or disk (or maybe you still have it in memory). Insert the following two lines:

```
575 IF B<36 THEN GOTO 725
725 PRINT "WIPEOUT!"
```

This will be a simulation of a stock purchase on 10% margin or a commodity purchase at 10% margin (precious-metals dealers are making this offer all the time). What this program does is print "WIPEOUT!" whenever your initial stake has gone to zero. Remember from earlier chapters that the whole point of a margin purchase is leverage; you get the whole impact of a price change by making a sort of "down payment." If the $40 stock or whatever goes to $44 you will have doubled your money; if it goes to $36 your account is wiped out (you may think of this as a $4,000 account on a $40,000 contract—if the whole contract goes to $44,000 you get to keep the whole $4,000 extra, but on the other hand, if it goes down . . .).

The wipe-out point here is set at the time when you would get a notice from your broker saying that you have been cleaned out. Assuming you are not a masochist, that your confidence in your judgment is not icily absolute, or that you have dependents who want to eat next week and who look to you for sustenance, you will ordinarily clear out under these circumstances to lick your wounds in private.

Here are ten sample runs produced by this program.

37.056	WIPEOUT!	37.6671	49.0761
38.4557	42.0616	35.3526	46.143
36.7963	41.5438	WIPEOUT!	47.8596
37.812	43.3334	37.5888	45.8895
36.2257	45.7979	37.1436	48.3587
36.5286	48.7581	34.4437	48.4624
39.0651	46.6181	WIPEOUT!	50.4266
40.2027	43.7996	41.454	51.3496
40.0956	40.8563	41.8123	49.4569
39.2814	38.295	44.7781	47.1324
37.5073	35.5841	47.037	45.7531
35.1262	WIPEOUT!	44.4018	43.4322
WIPEOUT!	37.443	42.346	40.7752
40.3104	35.6634	41.0487	38.216
37.8657	WIPEOUT!	43.1906	36.8408
37.2476	38.8282	41.4963	39.2386
36.9334	39.8942	41.7611	39.0458
35.2825	37.7057	40.5036	41.2862
WIPEOUT!	40.7014	42.0648	40.7243
37.9913	42.7076	39.7563	43.4523
35.2163	41.9149	41.7485	42.3469

WIPEOUT!	41.344	44.4072	43.123
37.3108	42.3894	44.7785	44.5854
36.8216	39.7154	47.5863	44.1338
34.0853	41.7187	49.6101	41.8327
WIPEOUT!	38.7427	49.8281	40.3462
38.0998	38.8198	49.8495	38.6645
37.8789	37.5596	51.7709	37.5257
36.3172	39.4561	49.2783	35.5139
35.0108	40.0198	49.0412	WIPEOUT!

It is realistic to assume that in two of these cases you would have had the judgment, and the time, to have taken a profit and laughed all the way to the bank (you could consider the time steps here to be weeks to get a feeling for how this works). In the other eight cases it is fair to say that the market would have scorched you to a crisp. And as you stand there, staring down at your little fried socks, think about this: *you may even have been right about the ultimate market direction. It just doesn't help.* It is a coincidence that out of ten runs you lose in eight. The reason it is a coincidence is that this is a perfect match to the statistic that 80% of small investors trading in commodities lose money. If you run this program one thousand times (that's a nice thing about home computers—computer time is free) you will find that maybe you could clear out with actual profit perhaps 40% of the time, but this hinges on your being able to move instantly to take, in many cases, fairly paltry profits. Therefore, unless you have nerves of steel and very, very deep pockets, all trading of anything on margin should be considered unacceptably risky. As we shall see in a later chapter, the recent spate of real-estate hyperinflation has made even the humble single-family dwelling a tricky margin speculation in some areas.

Forecasting and Other Shady Activities

The notion of a random walk, as presented above, has a long and honorable tradition in many areas of physics, chemistry, and biology. So that you won't have to die ignorant, the case of margin trading you just looked at is called a "random walk with absorbing barrier." There are random walks with two absorbing barriers, random walks with one or two reflecting barriers, random walks with statistical homing tendencies about a point, random walks in two, three, and more dimensions, and lots of other mathematical curios.

There are other topics borrowed from the world of experimental science into economics, and some of these have much less forceful claims for applicability. Because you are reading a chapter on stocks and so forth in a computer book, we are going to show you two examples of mathematical forecasting of the type found in all other computer books on investing and available for your delectation from many sources on disk packages costing between $200 and $600. Our claim to novelty is that we intend to show that these forecasting procedures are in general damnable nonsense, that they are believed only because their mathematical basis is improperly explained, and that they represent an entirely illegitimate borrowing from a method that is valid only in the real physical sciences for real physical data. One of the authors got to spend half an hour listening to someone at a cocktail party with this edifying tale to tell (you can get trapped waiting for the bathroom): it seems this guy had bought a forecasting package for the IBM PC and had run up the numbers on a favorite company, and had concluded from the forecast that he was going to make a bundle on this particular stock, *even though two of the officers of the company had just gone to jail and trading in the stock had been suspended.* He figured when trading started up again the stock would take off just like the forecast curve on his dear old PC. It would take more patience than is ordinarily available to explain what is wrong with this fellow's assumptions and mathematics, so the reader can puzzle this one out as homework.

Linear Regression

The nice thing about linear regression is that it sounds authoritative, that you can mention having done a linear-regression analysis of something and it sounds like something profound must have occurred. What is somewhat less nice about it is that it doesn't necessarily mean anything when applied to economic rather than physical data (sometimes it does mean something, but here we are going to confine our attention to stock prices).

Figure 6B Regression Analysis of Nonsense Data

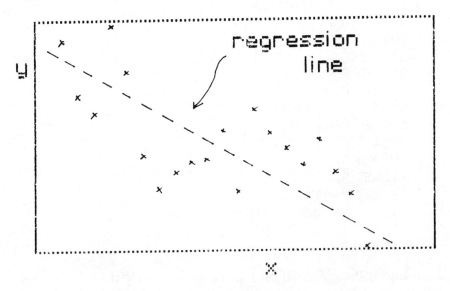

If you have a fuzzy plot of some data points, such as that shown in Figure 6B, a linear regression program will tell you how to draw a straight line through them. The straight line will be a "best fit" in the sense that it minimizes the distance of the points from the line. There are many other fitting methods, but this is the simplest, and in the cases we will be considering, no higher-order methods really apply anyway.

Program 6B performs a linear regression analysis on only twenty equally spaced points such as those in Figure 6B. Not only is it easy to find general-purpose linear-regression programs written in BASIC from dozens of other books (these programs are all much longer than this one), but with about $12 you can go out and get a calculator that does the same thing with little special keys. But here is this humble version:

PROGRAM 6B
Straight Line Through Buckshot

```
120 DIM Y(20)
150 PRINT "START INPUT"
```

```
200 FOR K=1 TO 20
250 PRINT "POINT ";K
275 INPUT T
300 LET Y(K)=T
350 NEXT K
400 LET S=0
450 LET P=0
500 FOR K=1 TO 20
550 LET S=S+Y(K)
600 LET P=P+Y(K)*K
650 NEXT K
700 LET S=S/20
750 LET P=P/20
800 LET A=(10.5*P−143.5*S)/(−33.25)
850 LET B=(10.5*S−P)/(−33.25)
900 PRINT "A=";A;"B=";B
```

SAVE Program 6B on tape or disk as LINREG (for linear regression), because there are suggested uses for it in a minute. We will try this program on the data in the fuzzy plot and see what kind of a line it produces. Saving you the trouble of data entry and rounding the input data and output data to two decimal places, the result is

$$A = 40.58 \quad B = 0.27$$

What are you supposed to do with this? Well, this tells you that the best straight line through the plot is the line

$$Y = 40.58 - 0.27 * X$$

that is, the form $Y = A + B * X$, with the value churned out by the program. We plot this through the data by taking $X = 1$ and finding that $Y = 40.31$ and putting this as an X on the chart; then we take $X = 20$ and get $Y = 40.58 - 0.27 * 20 = 35.18$ and putting this Y value on the chart at the appropriate spot.

As you inspect "the fit of the regression line to the data (ahem)" you will see that it looks fairly good. There is just one problem, but it is indeed a thorny one: *this data is the first random-number sequence generated by the random-walk program. The line can't predict anything because the underlying process is random.*

The hope in forecasting is that you would find out from

Figure 6C Real Stock Charts (courtesy of Daily Graphs, Wm. O'Neil &
Co., Inc., Los Angeles)

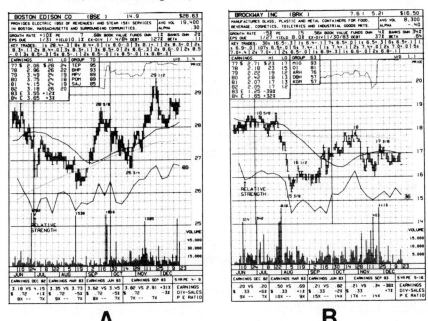

A   **B**

your analysis what happens next. This procedure, however just
finds a straight line through the data. This would allow you
to predict a Y value that corresponds to the next X (this would
be data point 21) if the data referred to a physical process in
which there was a law connecting Y and X. To say that this
means something as a procedure in stock forecasting is equivalent to saying that stock prices have a known, determinable
evolution in time. That is just _____ (fill in your favorite
synonym for nonsense).

One of the really interesting things to do is to apply this
program to historical pieces of stock data, taken 20 points at
a time. Figure 6C shows two six-month plots to discuss in
this context.

In plot A, you can pick a three-week chunk in which a
regression analysis predicts the stock price soaring into the
ozone, whereas in fact the stock was very shortly headed for
the mud. Likewise, in B, it appears that the stock is in crash-
and-burn configuration, but actually it is about to turn around.
Perhaps the most convincing demonstration of the inapplicabil-
ity of this method to price situations lies only in attempts at

application. If after the next section you need further convincing, go out and buy any package of programs that claims to be useful in stock-market forecasting. Then apply it, not to your current potential favorites, but to stocks selected at random in the first nine months of the previous year and see how well it forecasts the final three months of that year. Unless the market year under consideration is a total disaster or an absolute boom, it is a fair bet that the program will prove marginally better than divination among sheep entrails as a forecasting tool. And don't let anyone convince you that miracles can be performed with mathematical methods that are too complex to be explained; even economics deserves more respect than that.

Advanced Forecasting for Skeptics

"But golly, Professor, for sure all these distinguished savants must know *something* I don't!" you may find yourself muttering under your breath. Perhaps they do, but they don't know the price of Chrysler stock next year any better than you do. We will look this prospect over with the help of yet another program, also a standard item in the repertoire of forecasters. This one is called "exponential smoothing of time-series data" and is designed to give a relatively plain curve as a replacement for the now traditional fuzzy plot. In this sense it is an improvement on the straight-line program offered above, but unfortunately there just isn't any real basis for assuming that it can predict stock prices. Soldiering bravely on, we will nonetheless type it in for the sake of completeness in analysis. This is an abbreviated version of exponential smoothing that calls for only ten data points equally spaced in time.

Note, by the way, that Figure 6C (A and B) also includes some smoothed data—the solid line that runs through the stock prices is a *moving average.* The moving average is calculated by taking the average price over fixed time periods; today's moving-average number is, say, the average price over the last thirty days. The exponential-smoothing program (Program 6C) amounts to a belief that the moving average is a predictor of a trend.

PROGRAM 6C
Data-smoothing

```
100 DIM Y(10), Z(10)
125 PRINT "WEIGHT=?"
135 INPUT W
150 PRINT "START INPUT"
200 FOR K=1 TO 10
250 PRINT "POINT ";K
275 INPUT T
300 LET Y(K)=T
350 NEXT K
375 Z(2)=Y(1)
400 FOR K=3 TO 10
450 LET Z(K)=Z(K−1)+W*(Y(K−1)−Z(K−1))
500 NEXT K
550 PRINT "PREDICTION=";Z(10)
```

So that you can get some feeling for what's going on with this program, we will apply it to the fourth random-data set presented earlier. The program asks for a "weight," which must be entered as a number between zero and one—zero damps out all fluctuations, and the predicted value is whatever started the series, and one returns predicted values that are as twitchy as the original data (that is, unsmoothed). Entering the first ten numbers from the fuzzy plot, we find the computer returning a predicted next value of 38.87, compared to the actual value of 37.51 (numbers have been rounded off to two places after the decimal). This looks interesting but actually is not. The smoothing just takes any downward or upward trend at face value and predicts a number in accordance with the trend.

If stock prices really had momentum, like a car rolling downhill or an artillery shell fired in the air, this perhaps might mean something. In fact, much of the research on smoothing of time-series data was inspired by problems with tracking anti-aircraft guns in World War II. But statistically, stock prices don't act like slightly dodgy fighter planes; they act like pollen in a water drop, and all the smoothing in the world can't mask it. The smoothed data could have been generated in the first place as an equivalent random walk with different timing and step size; the main point is that the smoothing has no intrinsic

predictive value. Once again, the most convincing demonstration is to apply this program to known records of particular
stock and see how much predictive value emerges. Please feel
free to try out different weights in the program as well.

An interesting exercise is to compare accuracy of prediction (just of direction in the next step) in the cases of random
walks and on real stock records. If stock prices can be predicted
from charting techniques (this is an example of a simple kind
of charting technique), the smoothing program should work
notably better on real stocks. That is, it's supposed to be able
to detect a real movement against a background of jumpy
"noise." You will find, for example, that it gives some success
in a uniformly rising market. That, however, is not what you
want to know—what you want to know is when the market
is about to change direction. But the smoothing technique says
the market never does change direction. And *there* is the catch.

A Candle in the Darkness and a Fish in a Bag

There must be some hopeful conclusion to be drawn from
this melange of mathematical gloom, and there is. Obviously,
stock prices cannot be completely random, because they do
not, among other things, assume all possible values. So if you
are patient for a few more pages and can wade through a
few tall tales and some statistics presented only in pictures,
we have a method for you to ponder. The essence of this method
has to do with the source of nonrandomness in prices, that
is, the fact that there are real companies behind the stocks
and that there are real investors who must make the buy/
sell decisions.

We will take up these two points in order. To highlight
the issue we wish to discuss, we present in Table 6A a little
chunk of stock table (this one is from the fall of 1984).

The parts about high and low prices for the day and closing
prices are certainly comprehensible enough, but the part about
P-E ratio may not be immediately obvious to the uninitiated.
The P-E ratio is the price-earnings ratio, which is the price
of the stock divided by the company's earnings per share. The
number on this particular day for Rubbermaid ("Rubrmd" in
the table) is 16. You will hear this quoted as "Rubbermaid is

Table 6A A Little Piece of Stock Table

Yearly High	Yearly Low	Stk	Div	Pe	Sales 100s	High	Low	Last	Net Chg.
37⅞	23	ReichC	.60	10	238	32⅜	32	32	− ¼
5¼	3¼	RepAir		11	4640	5	4½	4⅝	− ⅛
2¼	1⅛	RepA wt			386	1¾	1½	1⅝	+ ⅛
40⅜	25⅞	RepCp	.60	8	403	40⅜	39⅞	39⅞	− ⅛
45¼	31½	RepNY	1.60	7	424	38⅝	36¾	37¼	− 1⅝
20¼	17½	RNY pf	2.12		10	18	17⅞	17⅞	− ⅛
26	20¾	RNY pfC	3.12		7	23⅞	23⅜	23⅜	− ⅝
58⅜	52	RNY pfA	6.60e		210	53½	53	53½	− 1
52¾	40	RNY pfB	3.08e		100	45	44¾	45	+ ½
36⅝	21½	RepBk	1.64	8	866	30½	30	30⅛	+ ⅛
30¾	20¼	RepBk pf	2.12		69	26½	25¾	26½	+ ½
18¼	13¾	RshCot	.32	30	191	17½	17	17½	+ ⅛
37½	23¼	Revco	.80	12	6730	30¼	28½	29⅝	+ 1
13⅞	9¾	viRever			82	10⅝	10	10½	+ ⅜
40⅞	28⅝	Revlon	1.84	12	8201	37¼	35½	37	+ 1
23	20	Revln pf			2	22	21½	22	
24¼	18⅜	Rexhm	.70	8	110	20	19	19	− 1
20¾	12¾	Rexnrd	.40	19	227	16½	16⅛	16⅛	− ½
68¼	52⅞	Reynln	3.20	9	11602	67⅛	65	66⅞	+ 1¾
48	45¼	Reyln pf	4.10		132	47¾	47½	47¾	
106¾	100½	Reyln pf			8	104	103⅝	103⅝	− ⅛
41⅝	26	RevMtl	1.00	7	1459	28¾	27⅞	28¼	− ½
88½	58¼	ReyM pf	4.50		19	62	61	62	+ ⅞
30⅛	24¼	RchVck	1.48	10	721	29¾	28⅛	29½	+ ⅝
34⅞	22⅝	RiegelT	1.80	36	50	27½	27	27⅛	− ⅛
62½	36¼	RioGran	1.60	16	6826	51⅝	50⅜	50½	− 1
26½	17½	RiteAs	.41	16	x5455	25⅝	22	25	+ 1⅝
35⅞	25	Robshs	1.00	7	377	30¼	29¼	29⅞	− ⅜
48½	38¼	Robtsn	1.60	14	170	42⅜	41¼	41⅜	− ⅞
29	12	Robins	.76	9	963	18½	17½	18⅛	+ ⅜
18¼	12¼	RochG	2.04	5	451	17	16⅜	17	+ ¼
32¾	27½	RochTl	2.28	9	x721	32⅜	31⅝	31¾	+ ½
34½	23	Rockwl	1.00	9	4285	29	27⅞	28⅜	− ¼
78¾	48⅛	RohmH	2.00	9	1277	61¾	59¼	61⅝	+ 2⅜
45	27	Rohrln		9	1150	43¼	41½	43	+ ⅝
16	10⅞	RolCmn	.10e	21	723	14⅛	13¾	14	+ ¼
17¾	9⅛	RolinEn		23	1565	17⅛	16½	16¾	
13½	6⅞	Rollins	.46	14	494	9⅛	8¾	8⅞	− ⅛
66⅝	28¾	RolmCp		45	10204	u66⅝	66¼	66⅜	
6⅛	2⅞	Ronson			90	3⅝	3½	3½	
25¾	12⅝	Roper	.64	6	555	16	14½	16	+ 1¼
34¼	25¼	Rorer	1.08	14	2842	30½	29¾	29¾	− ¼
14⅝	8¾	Rowan	.08		4724	11⅞	10¾	11⅝	− ⅛
54⅝	41¼	RoylD	2.87e	4	10761	51½	50	50	− 1¼
46¾	32⅝	Rubrmd	.84	16	985	39¾	38⅝	38⅝	− ⅛

Yearly High	Yearly Low	Stk	Div	Pe	Sales 100s	High	Low	Last	Net Chg.
42¼	31½	SCM	2.00	10	1371	41⅛	38¼	40⅝	+ 2¼
42½	23⅞	SFN	1.28	17	2023	u42½	41½	42⅛	+ ½
11⅜	7¼	SL Inds		11	88	11	10⅝	10⅞	
30	17	SPSTec	.72	16	223	26½	25⅜	26⅛	+ ⅛
26	15½	Sabine	.04	21	1389	18¼	16¾	18¼	+ 1¼
24	18¾	SabnRy	2.91e		x264	21⅜	20¼	21⅜	+ ⅝
19⅞	11⅜	SfgdBs	.24	15	498	14⅞	14	14⅜	− ¾
9⅝	5¼	SfgdSc			647	9	8½	8⅝	− ⅛
2⅞	¼	SfgdS wt			73	2¼	2⅛	2⅛	− ⅛
41¾	29	SafKln	.40	19	1093	39⅜	35¾	38	− 1⅛
29¼	21¼	Safewy	1.60	8	5144	26	24¾	25¼	+ ½
35¾	24⅝	Saga	.44	13	878	32⅜	31⅜	32⅛	− ⅛
18⅛	14⅝	StJoLP	1.60	6	122	18⅛	17⅞	18	
10½	9	SPaul	1.20		212	9⅞	9½	9⅞	+ ⅜
56¼	28⅝	StRegis	1.12	20	3297	53	51	52⅞	+ 1⅝
12½	6½	Salant	.30i		59	7¼	7	7¼	+ ¼
32⅞	21	SallieM	.11	17	3476	30½	29¾	30	− ¼
52¾	49¼	SallM pf	3.97e		2021	52⅛	51¾	52⅛	+ ⅛
22	17⅝	SDieGs	2.10	7	1466	21⅜	20¾	21⅜	+ ½
11¼	7½	SJuanB	.85e	11	1041	8¾	8⅛	8⅝	+ ⅜
10⅞	8½	SJuanR		16	181	10⅜	10	10	
61	35¼	Sandrs	.56	19	2946	43	40⅜	42¼	− ⅝
24⅜	18¾	SAnitRt	1.84	13	72	21⅜	20¾	20¾	− ¼
27	20¼	SFeSPn	1.00	10	11325	26⅛	25⅛	25½	− ½
34¼	24¼	SgtWel	1.32	16	13	32⅜	32	32	
16¼	12⅞	SaulRE	.20	40	30	15½	15⅜	15½	+ ⅛
17½	13¼	SavElP	1.60	6	238	17½	16⅞	17½	+ ⅜
18⅜	14¼	SavE A	1.34		10	u18⅜	18	18⅜	+ ½
11⅛	9⅝	SavE pf	1.28		13	10⅞	10⅜	10¾	+ ¼
8⅛	3⅝	Savin			1174	7⅝	6¾	7⅛	− ⅝
12⅝	8½	Savin pf	1.50		x23	11¼	10½	10½	− ⅝
44⅜	33	SchrPlo	1.68	10	3626	34¾	d33	34½	− ⅛
56½	37¼	Schlmb	1.20	12	19371	45⅞	43⅛	44½	− 1⅛
16⅞	7¼	SciAtl	.12	18	2184	8⅞	8⅛	8⅞	+ ½
32⅞	19¼	Scoalnd	.76	11	2353	24	22⅝	23⅞	
12⅞	6¾	ScotLad	1.18t	5	465	7⅛	6¾	7	− ¼
58	39⅞	ScotFet	1.80	28	5922	56¼	53⅜	54¾	+ ¾
34⅞	25¼	ScottP	1.12	9	1751	30⅜	29⅜	30	+ ⅛
16¾	11⅜	Scottys	.52	10	310	14⅝	13¾	13⅞	− ⅝
30⅞	20⅛	Scovill	1.52	9	1803	25⅛	23¾	25⅛	+ 1
29⅛	18⅛	SeaCntn	.42	7	318	27⅛	26½	26¾	+ ⅛
11¾	9½	SeaCt pf	1.46		133	11⅛	10⅜	11	+ ⅜
15	12⅛	SeaC pfB	2.10		110	14	13⅜	13⅞	+ ⅜
15⅛	12	SeaC pfC	2.10		208	13⅞	13¼	13¾	+ ¼
21½	14⅝	SeaLdn	.48		6533	19¾	17⅝	19¼	+ 1

selling at sixteen times earnings." Safeway, as another example, is selling at a P-E ratio near 8.

The P-E ratio represents some measure of the strength of the stock and the ability of the company to pay attractive dividends. At a P-E ratio of ten, for example, the company could afford, if it so desired, to pay out dividends that were 10% of the value of the stock. This would leave nothing left over for capital improvements and so forth but would have at least the spectacular effect of offering a better yield (at the time of this writing) than is available for most bank accounts.

Companies do not usually have to offer yields comparable to bank interest on their common stock, so they don't. Companies do, however, like to think of themselves as being able to earn at least as much money by doing something as they could if they deposited their entire capitalization in a bank. Thus, there is a tendency for the P-E ratio to have some relationship to interest rates. A P-E ratio of 1 is highly unrealistic, and a P-E ratio of 100 means that a stock is flying relatively high compared to the balance-sheet performance of its company. Please note also that these considerations are pretty much peculiar to American practice; Japanese and European companies face a somewhat different set of financial circumstances.

Sometimes when a stock really takes off (the stock in the Mississippi Company, mentioned in an earlier chapter, is a nearly perfect example) it sells for a very high multiple, that is, a very high P-E ratio. Every boom market has standout stocks that are speculative darlings for a while; these can be tricky to own when the zooming phase slows down. Here is a little tale, ostensibly about fish, but in fact about stocks that sell for a high P-E ratio. Given that the authors know hundreds of homely parables on economic themes, you are asked to marvel at their restraint in telling only one such story every three chapters or so.

It seems that a man walked down ten miles from his mountain village to a dock on the river, and there he bought eight fish for 10 cents apiece. The fish were wrapped in black plastic bags, which struck him as peculiar, but he went on his way. Soon he came to a little stand with a sign that read "We buy fish—25 cents each!" He thought, "Why not run a little return on my errand?" and sold one fish. Trudging onward, he came to another stand, with a sign offering 50 cents per fish; once more he sold one. As he climbed back toward the village he saw offers for $1, $2, $4, and finally, nearest his house, a sign offering $32 for a fish! He decided then that he had made enough money anyway, and figured it would be rather a treat to make a dinner of such a costly dish. So he opened the last bag and to his shock and horror found a foul-smelling fish head and a few bones. He then ran back down to the dock, found the fish seller, and screamed, "What do you mean selling me this kind of garbage to eat?" The fish seller screamed back, "You idiot! Those fish aren't for eating! They're for *resale!*"

We are concerned here with fish for eating. There are many companies with different levels of economic performance, different levels of stock attractiveness, and thus different P-E ratios. Like so many measurable quantities in this world, the P-E ratios of stocks show an orderly distribution, a modified version of the familiar *bell-shaped curve*. The distri-

Figure 6D Distribution of Real Stock Prices

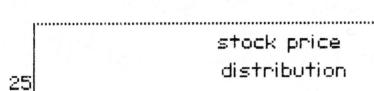

bution is not exactly the perfect theoretical curve, but Figure 6D shows, as a whimsical example, the histogram of P-E ratio stocks whose names begin with *S*, as they appeared on the New York Stock Exchange on one fine spring day.

The point here is that a company has more control over its earnings than it has over its stock price, so that the P-E ratio is subject to the same kind of random fluctuations as the stock price, but over a somewhat more limited range. In formulating our strategy, we will pay particular attention to stocks selling at below-average P-E ratios. This is also going to imply that we will be concerned only with companies that are currently making money. It may be that this restriction will cause us to miss out on some lovely opportunities, but we are actually just trying to improve our success rate over pure chance and are obliged to leave some of the more exciting prospects to the truly courageous (a polite way of referring to them).

The model that generates this profile of P-E ratios is a

Figure 6E Idealized Stock-price Distribution (See text for details of bargain-hunting in the Z-region)

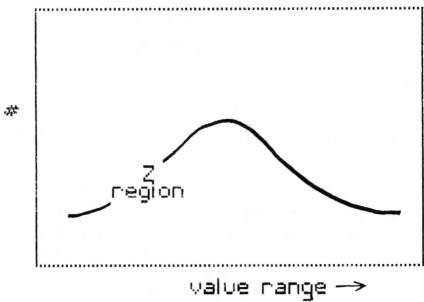

"random walk with reflecting barriers." It is a prediction of this model that if you start with a stock in region Z of Figure 6E, the path of that stock is somewhat more likely to cross the midpoint of the curve heading right than it is to end up to the left of where it started. This suggests the first element of the stock strategy:

Element one   Formulate a list of stocks whose P-E ratios fall around region Z in the distribution. (This point, technically, is one standard deviation below the average. We would emphasize this more, but many nontechnical persons think the expression *standard deviation* is faintly amusing.)

The same type of model gives a distribution of stock prices themselves that accords fairly well with what is observed. Figure 6F shows the corresponding plot for the NYSE *S*-stock shown in Figure 6E, on the same fine spring day.

Element two   The second element in the strategy is analogous to the first. Go over the first list and keep only those stocks whose price is in the Z-region. This should give you a much more manageable list.

Figure 6F Real P-E Ratio Distribution for a Stock Sample

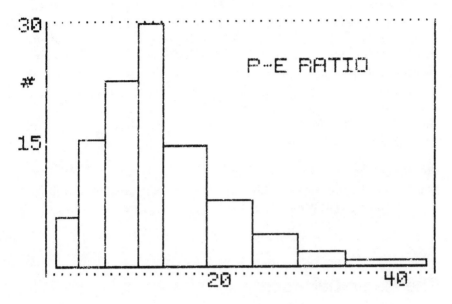

On the basis of these two considerations alone, with no examination of the companies involved, it was found for the year 1983 that stocks located in the Z-region on both figures had twice as good a chance of increasing by 40% or more than did stocks from the region on the other side of the central bump. What this suggests is something fairly straightforward: that in the thousands and thousands of individual investment decisions that go into the price of a given stock, there is a definite prejudice as to what constitutes a reasonable P-E ratio and what works out to be a reasonable average price for a stock. This prejudice establishes a weak "central drift" for prices, which tends to accumulate them around an average unless individual economic successes or failures drive them to the extremes.

Because there may be unpleasant reasons why a particular stock sells for a low price (although the method so far has eliminated those at alarmingly low prices—there aren't any of the often-interesting "penny stocks"), you may as well resign yourself to doing a little research. It helps to specialize in an industry group about which you know something. Typically this will not be this year's hot topic, for example, genetic engineering or robotics, but rather something related to your own job. It's amazing how much you know about the companies you have to deal with, even indirectly, compared to what you know about plasmid vectors or hybridomas if you're not a biologist. If the stocks that have emerged from the two screening processes don't have anything obviously wrong with them (don't worry, some of them will), you are then faced with your own decision. Thus we have the next element in this simple scheme:

Element three   Scan the list for companies whose fortunes you may be competent to evaluate. Remember, if you don't like any of them, you can always leave your money in a bank.

The Magic Dartboard

Probably anyone can understand enough plain English to read the information sheets on companies that are available at bro-

Figure 6G Ordinary Random-pick Dartboard

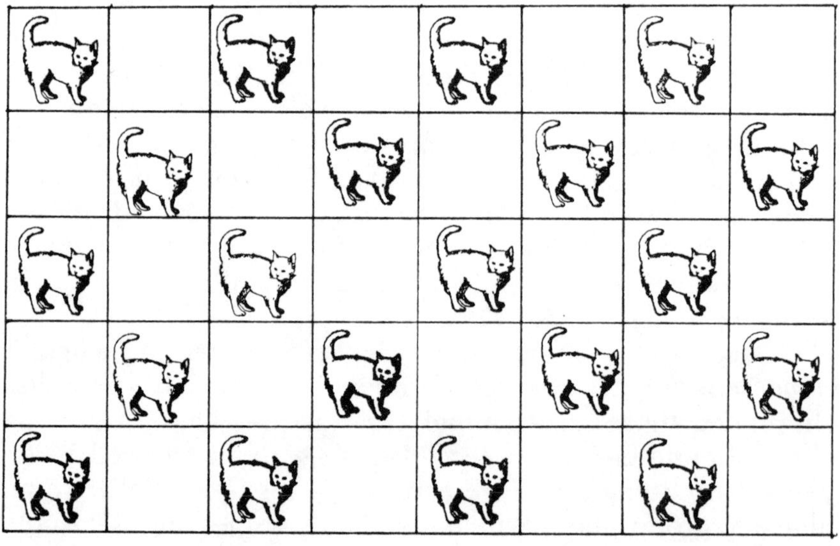

Figure 6H Statistical "Magic Dartboard"—Better Chances with Grouped
Targets

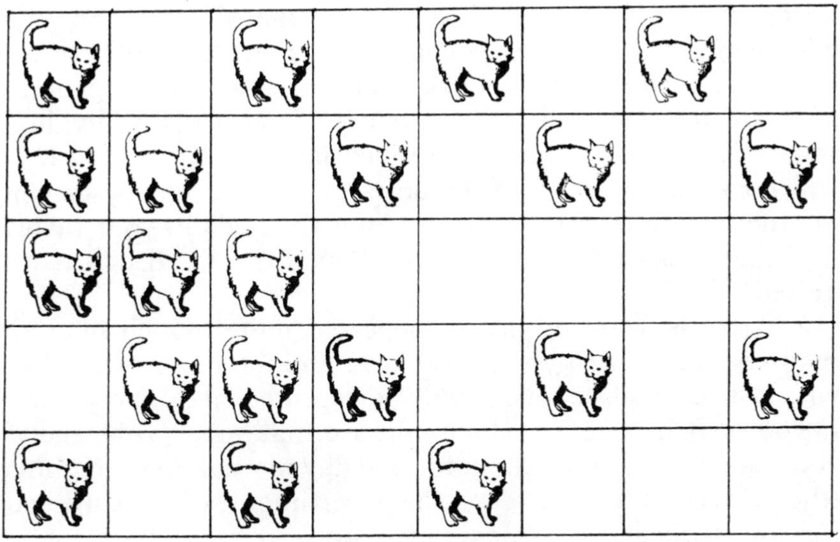

kers' offices, and most adults have enough residual paranoia
to do some reading between the lines (for example, if executive
salaries are two-thirds of a company's operating budget, watch
out). Statistics are another matter, so elements one and two
in our little strategy may require some explanation more vivid
than just the graphs presented. Here is an analogy that suggested itself in a jolly pub in the small town in which the
authors, for reasons of pure eccentricity, reside.

Figure 6G shows a Stock-Selection Dartboard as it is con-
ventionally understood, simplified to represent forty stocks,
neatly arranged in a 5 × 8 matrix. The checkerboard pattern
signifies that half of the stocks are going to go up and half
are going to go down (this describes a neutral market—in a
raging bull or bear market the percentage of cats vs. blanks
changes accordingly). You are given four darts, and the object
is to hit the cats. If you are standing far enough away, your
results should be very close to random.

Figure 6H is a picture of The Magic Dartboard. Here the
stocks have been selected by a statistical procedure so that
the left side of the dartboard has a preponderance of cat

squares. The checkering in this dartboard is approximately correct, for stocks chosen according to the criteria above for a six-month period in the mid-1980s during which the Dow-Jones average was nearly level (stocks that finished the year with less than a 5% price change were excluded). Now all you have to do is stand back, start tossing, and in general aim for the left side of the board. Instead of individual squares as targets, you have a much larger aiming area. It is still possible to land all four darts on blanks, but by grouping the cats in this way you have put the odds in your favor. And that is both the best one can hope for and all that is required.

There is also one last oft-repeated point, which may already be familiar to you if you have any interest in taxes but which, tiresomely enough, will be repeated here once more. If you have a stock in which you are making a profit and if you can stand to hold onto it for one day more than six months (the term used to be a year), the government will reward you for your forbearance by taxing you on your profit at only 40% of the rate you pay on the rest of your money. That's the secular miracle of long-term capital gains (these are 1984–85 rules, which should hold for some time). That's one of the reasons sane people are willing to bother with this often spooky area— that there are numerous possibilities for keeping more money than the typical bank account yields.

If (we sincerely hope not) you are losing money on your selections, you can close out these dogs in less than six months and take a short-term capital loss, which can be written off against your ordinary income up to $3,000 worth of loss per year (there are other conditions on this as well). Given the amount of money we feel the average reader has available for investment, this level of loss coverage should be adequate; after all, our rather conservative screening procedure is designed to weed out stocks that are headed for unmitigated disaster.

All this time you thought it was love that makes the world go 'round, and here it turns out it is the relative use of long-term gains and short-term losses. This interesting feature of the tax code can perhaps best be understood by means of a few examples and a program.

Let us suppose that you are in the 35% marginal tax

bracket (look back at chapter 4 if you have forgotten what this means, but in 1984 it was $30,000 in taxable income for a single taxpayer). This means that if you make $200 additional dollars by earning 10% interest on $2,000, you are going to be expected to hand over $70 to the IRS, leaving you with $130. On an additional $200 in stock-market long-term gains, you will pay taxes on only $80 of the $200, leaving you with $172. On the downside (as we say in the market), you will find that such frivolities as health insurance are practically nondeductible, but your stock-market short-term losses, up to $3,000, are subtracted from ordinary income. If you lose $200, you have really lost only $130 when taxes are taken into account.

Here is a little program that you can use as a guide to your prospects as a stock-market investor. Type it in and then save it with a suitable title (we are using TXBRK as an internal name) and then we will explain how to use it.

PROGRAM 6D
Tax Break on Stock Transactions

```
100 LET B=.35
150 PRINT "SUCCESS RATE= ? %"
200 INPUT P
250 PRINT "ODDS =";P;"/";100-P
300 LET P=P/100
350 LET G=P*1000*(1-B*.4)
400 LET L=(1-P)*1000*(1-B)
450 PRINT "EXPECTATION VAL."
500 PRINT "AFTER-TAX GAIN"
550 PRINT "= $";G-L
```

First, this program is set for the 35% marginal bracket in line 100; you should change it to your own marginal rate right now (and no excuses for not knowing this figure!). The success rate is basically your cat percentage from the magic dartboard, that is, the percentage of your selections that go up instead of down. Note that we give no attention to "short sales" in this book—if you know what these are you probably know there is no long-term-gains break on them, and if you don't know what these are, it may be just as well. The program assumes that you will ride a good position to a $1,000 long-term gain and a bad position to a $1,000 short-term loss. (See Chapter 9 for more details on this balancing method.) Of course, you may be a lot foxier than this, but the neutral assumption is made here to avoid putting too much faith in your luck.

The output of the program is the expectation value for your transaction. The expectation value in this simple case is

Expectation Value = (Probability of Winning) * (Amount Won)
    − (Probability of Losing) * (Amount Lost)

This is the statistical summary of your chances expressed as a dollar output. The concept of expectation value is very useful in probability and daily life. In a recent contest sponsored by a supermarket chain, the published odds showed a 1-in-485,434 chance of winning (contest tables are fascinating if you know what to look for) a prize of $10 in cash with a single game card. Thus your expectation value for the action of rubbing off the silver cover on the card is

Expectation Value = (1 IN 485,434) * $10
    = $0.0000206

To determine whether the time it takes you to rub off the silver is worth two-thousandths of a cent depends of course on your valuation of your own time; at the least this reinforces the feeling that supermarkets don't stay in business by giving away money.

The sample output, shown here for success rates of 40%, 50%, 60%, and 65%, is enlightening. Notice that at a 50% correct-selection rate you are already matching 9% bank interest, because these are after-tax figures. If you had earned $100 in bank interest, in your marginal bracket you would get to keep only $65. Perhaps the most interesting figure is that for a success rate of 60%. This gives a pretty healthy after-tax return and is by no means implausible as a success rate if you have the patience to go through the stock-screening routine suggested in this chapter.

SUCCESS RATE= ? %
ODDS = 40 / 60
EXPECTATION VAL.
AFTER-TAX GAIN
= $−46

SUCCESS RATE= ? %
ODDS = 50 / 50
EXPECTATION VAL.
AFTER-TAX GAIN
= $ 105

SUCCESS RATE= ? %
ODDS = 60 / 40
EXPECTATION VAL.
AFTER-TAX GAIN
= $ 256

SUCCESS RATE= ? %
ODDS = 65 / 35
EXPECTATION VAL.
AFTER-TAX GAIN
= $ 331.5

IRAs, Lifestyles, and So Forth

You have just had presented to you a pretty unexciting strategy, but one that has a great deal of statistical backing. In a total crash, you would probably be wiped out, but in a gently rising market you would have a portfolio that outperforms most other investments. Furthermore, this business of long-term capital gains is designed to promote a relaxed attitude. Far from watching the minute-to-minute results on a ticker or even consulting the Wall Street Journal every morning, you can probably get by using only the stock listings in your local paper on Sundays. Not included in the little program above is the delicate matter of brokers' fees; if you get too twitchy you won't really have to worry about long-term and short-term gains—the commissions will eat you alive. The strategy here is to pick long-term modest winners, avoid disaster, arrange things for maximum tax benefits, and not worry too much.

Things are a little different with a stock account in an IRA. Here your gains are not going to be taxed until withdrawal, so there isn't any point in observing the long-term (six-month) provision. Likewise, there is no effective loss cushioning from deductibility; if you lose $1,000, that's just a loss of $1,000, period. In an IRA, however, the strategy for selecting stocks is just the same. The strategy presented here is intended to be a method for selecting stocks that are somewhat undervalued, that represent basically sound companies in which there may not be much interest at the moment, and that have some headspace for price increase without sticking out too prominently. For an IRA, from the list you obtain by the screening routine, you might want to consider companies that pay out more of their earnings in dividends. In the plain strategy the emphasis is on long-term growth because that's where the tax advantage is. In an IRA, however, you can accept dividends without paying taxes. It is sometimes thought to be shortsighted for a company to pay out too much in dividends instead of reinvesting the earnings. You will have to judge for yourself how you think a given company should best manage its destiny. Perhaps you can find a company that pays enormous dividends (note that there is a partial dividend-exclusion feature in the 1984 tax code) and then bail out of its stock just before these profligate ways put them in the soup!

A Few Advanced Topics

We will now look at a few simple programs for evaluating the potential of some interesting stock-like objects; these are convertible bonds and options. They are called stock-like objects here because their value is related to the value of a corresponding stock. A company such as U.S. Steel, for example, is large enough and well-enough known to have a lively market in common stock (and preferred stock, for that matter), convertible bonds, and listed options. Many smaller companies do not support all three types of vehicle—never fear, some aspects of this will be sufficiently confusing that concentrating on a restricted list of companies is probably helpful.

  For both these topics we will consider only a fairly small subset of possibilities. So many new options markets have opened in the last ten years that another book the size of this one would be required to do justice to the vast number of maneuvers now available. Interest-rate options, foreign-currency futures options, and industry-group index options are only a few of the fascinating subjects we propose to ignore utterly here. There is some reasonably esoteric material to be extracted from ordinary stock options. Thus, without further delay we lurch forward into the basics of convertibles and options.

Convertible Bonds

A convertible bond is a security that pays interest income as a regular corporate bond does, but that can be converted to a fixed number of shares of stock. Because this conversion privilege has some possible value, a convertible pays less than a standard corporate bond issued by the same company. The value of a convertible bond, therefore, depends on both the difference in these yield rates and the implicit stock price in the conversion principle compared to the market price of the stock. This works out to be too many numbers for many average citizens to juggle, so convertibles are often overlooked, which creates a wonderful opportunity for investors who are willing to work their way through the arithmetic. As usual, we will try to get the computer to handle most of the tedious work, and we will try to get some perspective on the great attention that the sharpest professionals pay to these interesting securities.

Look in your newspaper in the financial pages; find the section on bonds, scan down the yield column, and notice all the bonds that say "cv" instead of listing a yield. These are the convertibles, and you will notice right away that they represent a much smaller universe than bonds, not to mention stocks. Believe us, if there were convertible bonds associated with every stock, you would have to spend the rest of your life computing red-hot deals. Anyway, you will find lines like this:

Bond	CurYld	Vol	High	Low	Close	NetChg
FLA 5½s90	cv	41	90	88½	88½	−1

This is the convertible bond issued by Fly-Low Airlines, our favorite transportation firm. The line means that the bond pays $55 on each $1,000 bond and that if you held the bond until its maturity in 1990 you would get paid back $1,000 as a bond holder. These days $885 will get you one bond; that's the meaning of the 88½ closing price (everything is stated as if the units were $100 instead of $1,000). The yield of this bond as a percent is now higher than 5½% because the bond doesn't cost $1,000 any more. The current yield is now

Yield = 5½/(885/1000) = 6.2%

This is not a spectacular yield at a time when ordinary bonds are turning over 11% or 12%. Thus we will have to look at the value of the bond as converted to decide if this investment is attractive. We go to the stock tables and find that FLA common stock is currently paying a dividend of $1.50 per share and sells for $42½. This is a yield of $1.50/$42.50 = 0.035 = 3.5%.

Now, if the convertible bond would convert straight across, that is, if your $885 in the bond market was worth as many shares as $885 would get you in the stock market, why would you ever buy the lower-yielding stock? You wouldn't, and that's why the bond isn't worth quite as many shares as you would get in the stock market. In effect, you are paying a charge in stock to compensate for the higher yield of the bond.

How many shares of stock would you get if you converted this bond? If you are clever in these matters, you will have noted that we haven't given you enough information to figure this out, and the information isn't in the newspaper either. You have to call a broker's office and find out what the conversion ratio, as it is called, was declared to be when the bond was issued. In this case the magic number is 17. If you calculate that in your $885 bond there are implicitly 17 shares, each share costs $52. Compare this to the quoted price of the stock above, and you will see that you are paying about $10 per share for the higher yield on the bond. Is this worth it?

To answer this we will use, as is our familiar custom, a program. Program 6E has as its output a number that is the index that traders use to decide if a particular convertible is a good bet compared to the stock. Please note that the convertible vs. the stock is the point of comparison; you should be considering the decision only if you have already decided that the company is interesting and that the stock is relatively a good value compared to other stocks (see the sermon on

P/E ratios earlier in this chapter). If the stock is overpriced, you shouldn't want the convertible.

PROGRAM 6E
Convert Index

```
 50 PRINT "BOND PRICE"
 75 INPUT B
100 PRINT B
125 PRINT "INT"
150 INPUT I
175 Z=I*100/B
200 PRINT I;"CUR YLD = ";Z
225 PRINT "STOCK PRICE"
250 INPUT S
275 PRINT S
300 PRINT "DIVIDEND"
325 INPUT D
350 Y=100*D/S
375 PRINT D;"STK YIELD =";Y
400 PRINT "CONV RATIO"
425 INPUT R
450 PRINT R
475 F=(B*10/R−S)/S
500 X=(F/(Z−Y))*100
525 PRINT "INDEX = ";X
```

This index turns out to be the number of years it would take for the superior yield on the bond to make up for the fact that it is a more expensive way to approach buying the stock. Note also that in general you wouldn't actually do the conversion after buying the bond; if the stock price takes off, it will drag the bond price up, too, and you could make perfectly respectable capital gains just by selling the bond.

In fact, the pattern has been that a 20% increase in stock price will produce about a 15% increase in the price of the convertible bond. On the downside, a 20% drop in the stock price will make a 10% drop in the bond, because the bond yield supports its price. There are exceptions to this, but it's true more often than not. Because of this the index value that means the convertible is a good buy is 4; an index of 3 means a great deal and an index of 6 means the stock is better than the convertible. These numbers represent a consensus derived from the experience of many bond traders.

The case of Fly-Low Airlines is instructive. Bond price is 88.5, "INT" is the 5½ (5.5) from the listing, stock price is 42.50, dividend is 1.50 and conversion ratio is 17. Put these in the program and you get an index of 8.38. In the specialized parlance of this sophisticated investment market, you would say that this stinks. These numbers, by the way, are the real numbers for a well-known company in the spring of 1984. At the same time, convertibles with indices from 1.8 to about 10 were available. There are some nice deals out there, and if you have the patience to look for them you will end up feeling very pleased with yourself.

The procedure that emerges from this takes three steps: a) find a stock that is attractive on the criteria established earlier, b) check to see if the company has any convertible bonds outstanding, and c) run the index test to see if the convertible is good relative to the stock. You should also try to check with an investment service that specializes in convertible bonds (Value Line has such a service) to see if there are any funny circumstances surrounding the bond; in some cases, if the stock price has risen significantly since the time the bond was issued, the company may be about to call the bond in for conversion. Aside from something untoward (and generally preventable) such as this happening to you, you should find that convertibles that index at 2 or 3 in the test above are better investments than the corresponding stocks. People avoid them because they seem complicated, but sometimes complication means opportunity.

The volume of trades in convertibles is so much smaller than that in stocks that the market is slightly trickier. You will usually have to give specific instructions to your broker to buy at a particular price rather than just sending him into the market with the name of some bond. If you get interested in convertibles, and the program listed here is really meant to motivate your interest rather than to explain the whole field, this and other trading specifics will probably be made clear to you in your first weeks of study. Again, don't overlook this market just because it forces you to acquire some specialized knowledge—that's what can give you an edge over other investors.

Beginning Options

Another "investment" that tracks the value of a particular stock is the option. It is definitely stretching the concept of investment to include options; these represent only the possibility of an investment and are themselves highly perishable. We are going to examine only listed options in stocks, although the options market contains every type of speculation imaginable.

Options may be either *calls* or *puts,* and for our purposes we will consider only buying them rather than writing (issuing) them. A call is a piece of paper that gives you the right to buy 100 shares of a stock at a particular price. When Fly-Low Airlines is selling for $42 per share in June, a $40 October call could sell for $400, meaning that the right to buy 100 shares for $40 in October sells for $400, usually represented as 4 in the listings in the newspaper. Two dollars of this is stock value (the stock is already at $42), and the other $2 is speculation. If the stock is selling for $50 as you head into October, the value of the option will probably be up around $1,100 or $1,200. You can either trade the option in the options market or exercise the option, that is, buy the promised stock at $40 per share and then sell the stock at a profit.

If good old FLA has, alternatively, crashed over the summer and is selling at $36 in late September, your option is now worthless; that is, the right to buy the stock for $40 is worth something only if the stock is selling for more than $40. You can thus make a potentially unlimited amount of money, and your losses are limited to the price of the option. Your losses will also include transaction costs, because you pay a commission on each trade and taxes.

For simplicity, in this discussion we will look only at the trade itself. The question in options is, does the unlimited gain times the gain probability exceed the limited loss times the loss probability? This is another expectation-value problem, and the answer in practice will depend on how well you have selected your underlying stock (be sure to check out Fly-Low's P/E ratio). Program 6F is a short program that will aid in this investigation.

The situation with puts, mentioned earlier, is the same arrangement upside-down. A put is the right to sell the stock at a given price, also with a time limitation as for calls (the time ranges from one to nine months after the present). When

Fly-Low is selling at $42, you will probably find a $45 October put selling for $400. This represents someone's heartfelt conviction that Fly-Low will be trading under $41 by October. If the stock sinks, the put is worth money, and if it goes past $45, the put becomes worthless. Because the situation is symmetrical to that for calls, and because we are mainly doing a conceptual exploration, we will make the program refer only to calls. In real life, we would caution, it is sometimes much easier to predict when a company will do poorly than when it will do well, making puts more appropriate. Also please observe that options have to do something in a very short amount of time—you can sit on your stock forever, but an option will die of its own accord in a matter of months, a tricky business of timing.

Program 6F takes the current stock price, the call label or "strike price" (here 40 is the label of the Fly-Low 40 October), and the option price to generate a little table showing your gain or loss depending on the subsequent price of the stock. This is set up so that the option price is entered as it appears in newspaper listings, that is, for a listing of 2¼ you type in 2.25 in response to the ? prompt. The action of the program is quite simple; it will be the table it generates that calls up a somewhat more sophisticated point.

PROGRAM 6F
Call-option Value

```
 50 PRINT "STOCK PRICE"
 75 INPUT S
100 PRINT S
125 PRINT "CALL LABEL"
150 INPUT C
175 PRINT C
200 PRINT "CALL PRICE"
225 INPUT P
250 P=P*100
275 PRINT P
300 PRINT "STK PRICE     VAL"
325 FOR K =1 TO 11
350 N=2*K
375 D=S+12−N
400 V=(D=C)*100−P
```

```
425 PRINT D;"        ";V
450 NEXT K
```

If you plug in the numbers for the case of Fly-Low (stock price = 42, call label = 40, call price = 4) you will get this for output:

STK PRICE	VAL
52	800
50	600
48	400
46	200
44	0
42	−200
40	−400
38	−600
36	−800
34	−1000
32	−1200

Remember that this stock is now selling for $42. If nothing happens, therefore, you lose $200. If the stock undergoes a pure random walk, with an equal probability of moving up or down, your expectation value turns out to be exactly this negative two hundred bucks. If you buy the stock and sit on it while it goes nowhere, you can perhaps collect dividends and have lost only the commission. With the option, if the stock doesn't move up, you lose the commission plus a zero-move penalty, in this case $200.

The reason people bother with this market is, among other things, that $200 is not so much money to lose. Instead of shelling out $4,200 for a hundred shares of FLA, you can bet the $400 option and bank the rest for six months. At 10% annual interest, you would earn enough on the remaining $3,800 to cover, after six months, about what you stand to lose on the average. This rather cautious market strategy has at least the always desirable goal of limiting losses while leaving possible profits open.

There are many more exciting and delicate maneuvers in the options market, such as holding puts and calls on the same stock at different prices or calls on the same stock at different expiration dates, but we sometimes suspect that these

techniques have been invented more for maximizing the number of possible commissions you end up paying than for any
more noble purpose (being "eaten alive in an alligator spread"
is one slang reference). We will leave critical evaluation of
these to a later work. In closing this section we would, however,
point out that if you cruise the options listings of your newspaper with this program, you will find that some options are
much more reasonable from an expectation value point of view
than others. Don't bother looking at one unless you think the
underlying stock has merit, but if you have a hot prospect in
mind, and it has traded options, by all means investigate.

Other People's Software: What's Worth Having?

It should come as no surprise that there is some very meritori-
ous stock-market software and some that will get you into all
sorts of fiscal trouble. The prejudice in this work is that forecasting software is usually not valuable, whereas information-
collecting/processing software is definitely helpful. Let us
clarify.

We are not saying, for example, that all stock prices are
random walks. Sometimes there are definite and real trends,
usually driven by news or by information that is about to become news. We are saying, however, that in many situations
the pattern of a stock's price is such a good mimic of a random
walk that you won't be able to tell a trend from a drift. Furthermore, all the technical forecasting software in the world won't
help you in this situation. Consider these points: a) if there
were a really good forecasting program, anyone could buy it
and invariably become rich; b) word-processing software guarantees you can write letters with it—do you know any forecasting software that guarantees you will make money?; c) it means
nothing that forecasting programs are sometimes right—in
fact, statistically, they simply can't be wrong all the time. The
managers of large mutual funds have access to the most sophisticated forecasting tools imaginable, and yet a great many of
these manage consistently to underperform randomly chosen
portfolios. What conclusion would you draw from this?

Information utilities, on the other hand, are great. Dow-
Jones, Standard and Poor's, Value Line, and several others

have information lines and associated software (sometimes you get a disk subscription instead) that will allow you to search for stocks according to selected criteria, such as price range or P/E ratio. Many of these services allow you to check out earnings statements and projections and to investigate a company's performance over the years. You could get much the same information with a subscription to Barron's (ought to have one anyway, if you're serious about this), but for those with a disk-based system with lots of RAM and a modem, the information services perform a tremendous convenience function.

In any case, don't let the availability of mountains of rapidly-sortable data lead you into trading too much. The best strategy for someone who has a real job and interests other than ticker-watching is to spend a reasonable amount of time studying a small number of situations and then take up positions that last long enough that the gains are long-term for tax-purposes. The transaction costs, even with a discount brokerage firm, will put your expectation value down in the mire if you jump around in the market every few weeks.

7
Insurance

Insurance has a strange place in a book on money strategies. In all the other chapters of this book, the idea is to maximize your possible gains, particularly after taxes and inflation. In this chapter, the idea will be to minimize what is essentially an expense that cannot always be avoided. Although the underlying basis of all forms of insurance is statistically the same, different forms of insurance represent different levels of personal consequence; however dreadful you may feel about having your car stereo forcefully removed, it just isn't in the same class as being run over by a truck.

Here is the fundamental proposition in insurance, using the car stereo reference to make it slightly less threatening. The procedure outlined will be that of an idealized non-profit insurance company that pays out all its funds in exact accord with probability. In modern American practice (to the companies themselves), we hasten to point out, "idealized" means institutions whose judgment is so acute that they never end up paying out a cent.

For the sake of argument, we will say that you live in a neighborhood in which there is one chance in a hundred that your car stereo will be ripped off in any given year. What is a fair price for insurance against this event? If the stereo is worth $400, the insurance company faces a 1/100 chance of a $400 loss; their expectation value is negative $4. Thus, if they have no internal costs and don't want to make money, they should charge you $4 for the insurance. That's the theory. Likewise, an idealized life insurance company, noting that you are a forty-year old male, would figure that you have about two chances per thousand of dying this year and would thus charge you $20 for a $10,000 life-insurance policy for this year only.

These two examples also point out the differences between types of insurance. In general, you can't even come close to the zero-profit version of car-stereo insurance. There are, however, term-life insurance policies that are at least within striking distance of the idealized life insurance model (one of the authors is lucky enough to have such a policy, administered by a fund for college teachers). These nearly ideal policies are quite rare. Real insurance companies, depending on the type of insurance and the style of the company, pay out claims at a rate of about 7% to 30% of the theoretical rate. There are examples of insurance companies, particularly those that write accident policies, that have succeeded in paying out exactly nothing for years. Apart from these notorious predatory cases, it may be noted that life insurance executives are among the highest-paid persons on the face of the planet, so the zero-profit, zero-cost model is not going to apply very often.

Before we begin producing programs for evaluating insurance expenses (please observe that we have the operating bias that we don't want you to get sick or robbed or killed), we should note that the areas of insurance that will call for programs—health and life—are centers of financial and emotional problems. Even the best-administered health insurance policies must take into account the nearly uncontrolled explosion of medical costs in the last decade. Although all sorts of schemes are currently being tried (health maintenance organizations are an outstanding example), it just ain't cheap to get sick.

Life-insurance practice must take into account the almost entirely emotional associations this topic has for most people. For generations Americans were sold policies on the basis of heart-tugging salesmanship rather than an understanding of costs and benefits, and it is not uncommon to meet older people who are very proud of what they saw as a sincere commitment to the security of their families. In many cases the policies they think of fondly were such a raw deal that they can't accurately be characterized in wholesome and instructive reading such as this. We will say the policies were disadvantageous, which is four to five times more letters than necessary.

In the real world, in which people have to take real risks and can earn real interest on their money, the classic whole-life policy popular since World War II represents in most cases a truly terrible investment. We will check this out in some detail, but it will be clear that these policies were generally bought with sentiment prevailing over understanding.

Health, Risk, and "Deductibles"

There is a simple application of the probability reasoning above, and it explains something about the price structure of health and dental insurance. Suppose you are definitely going to get two check-ups per year at $25 each. How much should the insurance company charge you for a dental policy with no deductible? They will at least have to recover the $50's worth of visits, plus their cost in processing the claims, plus a "real-insurance" amount that covers the prospect that the dentist might actually find something interesting and expensive in your mouth. Insurance to protect you financially in case it happens that all your molars have turned to sponge cake is a real function, that is, risk coverage. "Insurance" against a sure thing, for example, your inevitable office visits, is a different matter. This is analogous to policies that cover new eyeglasses and pregnancy, situations that, one hopes, more typically represent intention than accident.

The reason we are clattering on about this point in such an insistent way is that we have met few people who seem spontaneously to have absorbed it from life. Is it really a good deal to have a health policy that covers every bottle of aspirin you buy in a year? Many people think so, but we give you our word as gentlemen that any insurance company is going to collect the money from you in advance; alternatively, the money may be collected from your employer, who then has less money for you. Soon you will see a program to emphasize this, but the qualitative point, we hope, is clear anyway: you can't beat the insurance companies by collecting money on sure things—they'll see to it that they get their money plus a hefty inefficiency surcharge.

Program 7A is a demonstration of the problems inherent in asking the insurance company to buy your cough syrup. It calculates monthly and yearly insurance premiums for the standard major medical health policy of one of the best known national insurers, for a fairly expensive chunk of the West

Coast. If you are lucky enough to live in a much cheaper area, you will find that the whole rate table just scales up and down; in Amarillo, for example, just multiply the output by 0.7. The lesson will turn out to be the same for all regions.

PROGRAM 7A
Health Plan

```
 50 C=1
100 PRINT "ENTER AGE"
150 INPUT A
200 M=A*C*5.45
250 PRINT "DEDUCTIBLE CODE=?"
300 INPUT D
350 F=1
400 IF D=2 THEN LET F=0.7
450 IF D=3 THEN LET F=0.53
500 M=M*F
550 Y=12*M
600 PRINT "ONE YR. PREM =$";Y
```

This program is short because it contains some approximations and requires some input from you; it does, however, give premiums that are within a few percent of the actual numbers, especially if your age is in the middle of a decade range (the tables are set for ranges such as 30–39 and the program, for simplicity, plots things as if everyone in this range were 35). The deductible code used in the program is this : for $200 deductible input 1, for $500 input 2, and for $1,000 input 3.

Let's look at some sample output for the case of a standard family, with the head of household being thirty-five years old. This is the case listed explicitly for C=1 in line 50. The program also gives result for a single person (C=0.4), adults with no children (C=0.75), an adult and one child (C=0.65), and an adult plus two or more children (C=0.75). At any rate, for our little test family the program generates this table:

Deductible	Premium
$200	$2,289
$500	$1,602
$1,000	$1,213

Consider this carefully. Suppose this family makes it through the year with $100 in medical bills, for example, just routine check-ups for the kids. In this case, they have paid $100 + $2,289 in health care costs in a year in which nothing happened, assuming they have the $200-deductible plan. What if they had been hit with $600 worth of bills? They would have paid the $200 deductible and been covered (this is fairly standard) for 80% of the remaining $400, or $320. The bill for the year is then $200 + $2,289 + ($400 − $320) = $2,569.

If, in the same year, they had had the $1,000-deductible policy, they would have been stuck with the whole $600 tab but would have been paying only $1,213 in insurance for the year, for a total of $1,813. You may work out for yourself the consequences of larger and smaller medical expenses—the message is going to be the same.

The message is also the same for other types of insurance, for example, personal property and automobile damage insurance. If you want a policy that will pay off when your $29.95 Toast-R-Oven is removed from the premises by a scampish weekend guest, you will make payments that in a year could have bought you a grand piano. Likewise, if the comprehensive on your automobile insurance has a deductible so small that it covers theft of Kleenex from your glove compartment, the cost will be alarming. We hope that this conclusion is so obvious that you are picturing the authors beating a dead horse at this point. One of us, however, works for a firm at which the employees recently voted in a dental plan that costs $220 dollars per year and has a deductible limit of zero instead of a $40-per-year, $100-deductible alternative, on the grounds that "at least you get something back when you go for a check-up." So the horse we are beating is apparently not universally dead. The little thrill that people get from an insurance-company reimbursement check for ordinary services is one of the most expensive little thrills imaginable.

This Is an Investment?
Life Insurance by the Numbers

The preceding material is really more in the spirit of the earlier work *Basic Money*, which is concerned with minimizing your expenses to the point at which you actually have something to save. Insurance on anything short of your untimely exit from this vale of tears is regarded as a consumer expense, that is, an area in which you want the most effective coverage for the least money. (Actually, a bizarre variant that is a consumer "bet against death" is airport-vending-machine plane-crash insurance—statistically the worst bet you can find.) The interesting part of the insurance business has to do with life insurance and its role as an investment, or in many cases a noninvestment, for the average person.

We will take this in three stages: first, we will examine what insurance would cost based purely on your statistical chances of dying; second, we will present a small program that suggests the dollar amount of life insurance you should carry; and third, we will analyze the yield on the types of insurance that have a savings or investment component. It should be noted at this point that the period between 1978 and 1985 has seen sweeping changes in the life-insurance business. What most people understood by the expression *life insurance* in the 1950s and 1960s was generally the so-called whole-life policy. This type of policy is a combination forced-savings scheme with an additional pure-insurance component. Because of the savings component, this is the kind of insurance people can borrow money against; it has been losing popularity because the interest paid on the savings is lower than that on most other investments. The pure insurance referred to here is called *term insurance.* It is a straight bet, usually renewed each year, between you and the insurance company, on the odds on your demise. It has no cash value (because you don't put any extra money into it) and is worth something only if you die, but thereby provides much more coverage for an equivalent premium than does whole-life insurance.

Two plans that have emerged in the 1980s are universal life and variable life, both of which are variants on whole life in that they have a term-insurance component and a cash-reserve or savings component. The reason that insurance companies persist in offering these hybrid devices rather than straight term insurance is that they like to have large amounts of cash to play with—typically they make more money as investment income than they make on the risk/loss business. Furthermore, in most cases these policies carry fairly large commissions, so it is no problem motivating a sales force to go out and recruit these sources of investment funds (for example, you). Anyway, universal life puts the savings part of the policy in bonds that yield acceptable, if not spectacular, interest, whereas variable life takes the cash reserve into stock-and-bond funds selected by the insurance company. When we get to the program that analyzes the yield on these policies, it will probably become clear who should be interested in them and who should avoid then. Right now we will first concern ourselves with the mathematics of the pure-insurance case, a cheerful little calculation to determine your chances of dying.

Basic Insurance

Program 7B does not calculate the odds on your demise as such, but rather the amount you should expect to pay for pure-cost life insurance, in dollars per thousand dollars of insurance. Not by coincidence, this number is exactly your chance per thousand of shuffling off this mortal coil; that is, if the insurance is $10 per thousand dollars you have ten chances per thousand (expressed another way, one chance per hundred) of dying this year. The reason for this correspondence is the pure-cost part—the real insurance company offering you term-life insurance will be either close to this number, if their policy is a bargain, or up to three to four times higher, if they are more predatory. In either case, the number represents the cost to the company of the risk involved. This will all become clearer, if it is not already, when we look at a sample of program output.

PROGRAM 7B
Term Life " *term life* "

```
 50 C=1
100 PRINT "ENTER AGE"
150 INPUT A
200 PRINT A
250 V=(A−35)/35
300 V=V*V
350 T=1.2+21*V+8*V*V
400 PRINT "TERM LIFE PER $1000"
450 T=T*C
500 PRINT "=$";T
```

This program is a reasonably close fit to the tables of actual mortality statistics; in its worst case it gives the figure correct to within 50 cents or so from ages twenty-five to sixty-five. If you are between the ages of sixty-five and eighty-five, first we wish to congratulate you and wish you many years of happy computing, but we must also ask you to change line 350 to

```
350 T=21*V+8*V*V+4.1*V↑4
```

in the interests of accuracy.

The tables reflect the mortality statistics for men. If you are a woman, change the index in line 50 from 1 to 0.67; this is one of the few breaks you can expect in life, so grin as you change it. If you are a worse-than-average health risk, for example, grossly overweight, alcoholic, or prone to cleaning loaded revolvers, change this index from 1 to 2. Believe it or not, this is quite a good approximation. If you are a fat, alcoholic, female gun freak, the index probably goes to 1.35, but you probably ought to think about changing your lifestyle as a priority over computing these numbers.

What you should find, as you try a few examples, is that term insurance should be relatively cheap when you are younger and that the cost starts to rise rapidly around the age of sixty. A policy for $100,000 will cost about $200 per year when you are in your early forties and will rise to $21,000 per year when you are sixty. This is just the inexorable logic of mortality. It also contrasts with the more traditional way of packaging insurance in the U.S., in which you are asked to start making payments of $2,000 per year in your early thirties, with the promise that these payments will stay relatively constant over the years, for the same amount of insurance.

One of the things you may also observe is that it will be relatively inefficient for the insurance company to sell you a chunk of term insurance as small as $1,000. Given that it probably costs even the best-run company about $5 to send you a letter and a few more dollars for record-keeping costs, a reasonable minimum term insurance policy for someone in his thirties or forties would be $25,000, with $100,000 not unreasonable as a standard (for a policyholder at age forty that would be about $14 per month). If you want a tiny amount of coverage instead, the paperwork costs will be greater than the insurance-risk costs.

Very small policies are no bargain, and neither are policies with a "one-size-fits-all" price. A common form of this is the insurance sold on home mortgages. Although this kind of policy will pay off your mortgage if you die, in general the rates are linked to the size of the mortgage rather than to your own statistics, and for the same amount of coverage, straight term life policies are usually cheaper. You can see, however, why the bank that issued you the mortgage thinks this is a great idea; the insurance they write up for you is like a little bonus over and above the money they are making on your home loan.

Table 7A Sample Output of Program 7B

Age (male, standard risk)	Cost (per $1,000 of insurance)
35	$1.20
40	$1.63
50	$5.33
60	$14.00
65	$20.94

For reference, and for those too lazy to type in the program and run it, Table 7A gives sample output for a few selected ages. This table will be needed at two later points in this chapter; first, we will use it in the determination of how much to pay for the coverage we are about to calculate for you, and second, we will use it to factor out the risk-insurance-vs.-investment part of the whole-life (or variable or universal-life) type of plan. Determining your coverage level will prove to be one of the more philosophical parts of this otherwise rather unspeculative book.

How Much Insurance Is Enough?

Very few of the assumptions in old-time life-insurance rule-of-thumb calculations seem to be valid any more. The standard calculation usually assumes that the insured is a male head of household whose intentions are these: a) his wife must be supported to age 90 (we're quoting this from a handbook!)

without working, at the same income level; b) all children will
be sent to the most expensive private college available, all expenses paid; and c) the after-tax, inflation-adjusted yield on
an invested death-benefit lump sum will be about 3%. At the
moment, only part c) of this seems realistic, and the rest is
closer to a greedy insurance saleman's fantasy than it is to
social reality.

We are going to present two programs that are variations
on the standard financial guides for deciding how much insurance you need. After all, most of the advice you are likely to
get on this topic is generated either directly or indirectly by
life-insurance companies themselves. What we will try to do
is figure out what amount of money would provide a realistic
replacement income upon the demise of one adult in a partnership (the whole topic of insurance for anything but the official
Leave-It-to-Beaver, TV-type family almost never appears in the
brochures from insurers).

Before we do this, however, we may as well make explicit
the kind of assumptions which we think correspond to social
realism in the late 1980s:

- Nobody knows what's going to happen in the next forty years,
  so just plan for the next fifteen to twenty. All mature industrial
  economies are headed for a situation in which there are at
  most two workers per retired person by the year 2000 (West
  Germany, for example, will have a one-worker/one-pensioner
  social structure in ten years). There will be massive and dif-
  ficult-to-predict changes in Social Security, and anything
  you wish to use in a program now is guesswork pure and
  simple.
- Both adults in a household unit have to work, so the program
  will be neutral about whose income is being replaced. Most
  two-income families facing today's housing market would be
  blown out of their domiciles by the death of a spouse on the
  third mortgage payment after the funeral. The focus in the
  programs will be a consideration of housing as a principal
  expense, and the idea will be that replacement income for this
  is what the insurance should provide.
- The kids don't automatically go to Harvard if you croak. We
  are looking to provide enough income to replace your monetary function until they are old enough to fend for themselves.
  There is obviously a reasonable middle ground between leaving

your family in church-mouse poverty and leaving your spouse a Maserati with live-in mechanic. In these computations, your family won't suffer any hardships (other than the obvious emotional ones) but won't be doing any better than they were when you were around. The reason for this is that insurance is essentially a defensive measure, an expense to be minimized after you have decided on the right amount. You would be better off taking a few thousand dollars per year and plunging them into course work for job-skills upgrading for both spouses than shipping them to Nevernever Mutual Life every year. With the job-upgrade strategy, you can even derive benefits by not dying!

How Much Will They Need?

Program 7C calculates the income needed to make up for the loss of one income in a two-income family. One of the incomes could be zero, for generality; also, please don't worry that the program calls for "spouse's income"—the program works without a valid marriage certificate (we just had to call the entry something). The program assumes: a) the survivor will collect about $5,000 per year in Social Security benefits, an assumption that is predicated upon the presence of toddlers; b) that housing costs have been taken care of in the insurance settlement—you enter your old housing costs as a percent of your former joint take-home pay; and c) for "spouse income" you will put down a guess for the years ahead. There is also a standard factor in line 550 that subtracts your expensive tastes from the family budget.

PROGRAM 7C
Income Difference

```
 50 PRINT "TOTAL INCOME"
100 INPUT T
150 PRINT T
200 PRINT "HOUSING %"
250 INPUT H
300 PRINT H
```

```
350  PRINT "SPOUSE INCOME"
400  INPUT S
450  PRINT S
500  H=1-H/100
550  C=0.75
600  Z=T*H*C-5000-S
650  PRINT "INS DIFF PER YEAR"
700  PRINT "=$";Z
```

Try this case in this program: two incomes, husband—
$26,000 per year, wife—$14,000 per year, 20% of net income
spent on housing, husband dies. The program calls for a supplemental income of at least $5,000 per year. This seems somewhat
modest as a replacement for $26,000, but we have knocked
off both the housing expense and the cost of operating the
husband, as well as adding in some Social Security. If you
wish to take an extremely conservative approach, you can
change the index in line 550 to C=1, in which case you will
get $13,000 per year as the supplemental sum. Looked at out-
side the program, this gives the little family $32,000 per year,
a paid-for house, and no golf shoes or martinis to buy, so they
are probably well ahead of their old financial state. Thus, if
you are really nervous, change the index for your own case
to C=0.85 or so, but for the rest of our examples we will return
to the case C=0.75.

One interesting example to check is the untimely death
of the wife, in which case the program puts out negative $7,000
as the required income. That's because we have built in the
assumption that all housing costs are settled by insurance, that
is, the wife's insurance takes care of the outstanding mortgage
(or buys a house, if the family had been living in an apartment).
Some people may consider this case extreme, but it should
be noted that the wife in one of these situations has about
67% as much a chance of dying as the husband, and thus deserves some serious insurance-planning consideration. We will
give a short worksheet at the end of the chapter for looking
at various ways of doing this; the asymmetry in husband-vs.-
wife insurance is obviously induced by the inequality in male/
female pay scales, a phenomenon that will probably outlive
us all, unhappily enough.

Please also accept our assurance that the detached style

in which these matters are being discussed in this chapter does not connote flippancy but is rather an indication of the extreme difficulty that married persons with small children, for example, the authors, have in approaching these matters. This is why fathers have traditionally been classic suckers for really unfavorable insurance policies. This is a hard business to face, but unfortunately, a necessary one.

Let us look at two more standard cases. First, take a joint income of $30,000, housing expense of 15%, and spouse income of zero after the death. This could occur quite readily in a situation in which partners were helping each other with child care on very small children; after the death the parent wants to stay home with the children for a while. This example produces an income need of about $14,000 per year. Next we will take two people making $56,000 per year, neatly divided at $28,000 each, with a 25% housing expense. The program gives negative $1,500 as the need, showing the dramatic effect of covering the housing costs. If you run the same example with zero entered as housing percent, you get a need of $9,000 per year—that's an assessment of the amount of money one of these people was contributing to the mortgage.

The economic logic behind this partitioning, in which we will figure out the total insurance as one lump to pay for housing and one lump to provide replacement money for living expenses, has to do with interest rates. Unless you are very lucky, you are unlikely to find an investment that pays as much as a bank will charge you on a mortgage. Furthermore, because we are talking about long-term security, living in a building that is owned outright insulates the survivors from changes in interest rates in the future.

So the question becomes, if you already know you need $65,000 to pay off your mortgage or buy another house, how much more insurance do you need to provide $11,000 per year for fifteen to twenty years? That is exactly the subject of the next program.

Program 7D will just clunk along, paying you interest on a deposit and making annual withdrawals until the money is used up. It is possible to do a monthly version of this instead; the monthly version would be marginally more accurate but much slower to run. This program, although simple-minded, has the virtue that it is easy to modify. Type this program in and we will then discuss applications.

PROGRAM 7D
Yearly Returns

```
 50 PRINT "LUMP SUM"
 75 INPUT P
100 PRINT P
150 PRINT "YEARLY PAYMENT"
175 INPUT W
200 PRINT W
225 C=4
250 R=1+C/100
300 FOR K=1 TO 60
350 P=P*R−W
400 IF P<W GOTO 700
450 NEXT K
500 PRINT "OVER 60 YRS!"
550 GOTO 750
700 PRINT "ACCT FOR ";K;"YRS"
725 PRINT "BAL =$";P
750 END
```

This program has as an explicit parameter an estimated after-tax, after-inflation return of 4%, in line 225. The traditional number for this would be 3%, and a wildly optimistic number for it would be 7%. The reason that we feel that 4% is probably right for the near future (1985–1990) is that giant government deficits will be crowding the credit market, forcing up interest rates and in turn probably precipitating a recession. It will thus be a good time to be sitting on a pile of cash and a bad time to be working for a living. In any case, with a little fishing around it should be possible for the survivors to park the death benefits somewhere to get at least 4% real return. It might be possible to do better than this with aggressive stock-market work; this is, however, a well-known road to ruin for widows, orphans, and, one supposes, the occasional widower as well.

Try this case: see how long $80,000 lasts with $9,000 per year withdrawals. The program should give you eleven years worth of payments, and about $1,779 left at the end. Now, just for comparison, try a $120,000 lump sum with the same withdrawal schedule. The program tells you that the payments will last for nineteen years with a left-over chunk of $3,780.

The point here is that a 50% increase in the starting lump gets you much more than a 50% increase in the length of payments. If the starting lump is too small, the withdrawals will chew it up before the interest has any time to compound. Alternatively, try withdrawals of $4,500 instead of $9,000 on our original $80,000 lump. In this case you get thirty-one years of payments with a $2,873 final chunk. We summarize this in Table 7B to force home a conclusion.

Table 7B Sample Term-insurance Amounts and Payments

Lump	Pmts	#	Total (+ Rem)
$ 80,000	$4,500	31	$142,373
$ 80,000	$9,000	11	$100,779
$120,000	$9,000	19	$174,780

Just as buying small amounts of insurance (we are talking about term insurance here) is a bad idea because the service charges are large compared to the risk component, so small death benefits also work out to be not so hot, because they won't sit in an account long enough to accumulate much interest income. Compare the amount of extra money derived from the original benefits in the cases in which the payment schedule is extended over longer times.

Furthermore, when you are young and healthy, term insurance is relatively cheap. The time when you would presumably need to have a large death benefit corresponds exactly to this time. Later on, when you are past sixty and the cost of term insurance is rising rapidly, you just won't need, by any reasonable criterion, such a fabulous death-bonanza. This is one of the circumstances in which insurance can be seen as an extremely rational, socially beneficial concept. Just at the time when the loss of your income would produce the maximum hardship for your family, the rates are cheapest. Sometimes things work!

And sometimes they don't, which is a topic we will address in the next section. For now we will leave this part with a simple worksheet for you to use with the programs (see Figure 7A).

Here is an example of the use of such a worksheet. The easiest entry is probably the last—just figure out your current

Figure 7A Worksheet to Use with Life Insurance Programs

1. Figure per-year income-replacement need _____

2. Use Program 7C to get lump-sum equivalent _____

3. Enter housing purchase total _____

4. Add first-year expenses (funeral, consumer
   loans) _____

5. Add the last three numbers, and start shop-
   ping for the best price on term insurance
   for that total _____

credit-card and consumer-loan balance and add that to death expenses. We'll take $10,000 for this case. Now suppose the replacement-income figure is $7,000 per year, and you figure it will be needed for 20 years. Poking around with Program 7C will turn up the number $100,000 as the appropriate lump sum (just start with a trial number and adjust it until the payments last 20 years). Let us also figure that there is a $70,000 mortgage to retire.

This comes to a total of $180,000, of course. For a thirty-seven-year-old male, this amount of term life at the best current rates would cost $350 per year, and at not-so-hot rates, about twice that.

Ten years later, the price of this amount of term life would have doubled, but by then there would presumably have been some reduction in the mortgage, and the replacement income would have to last only ten years instead of twenty. Note also that the approach taken here makes a sharp distinction between risk coverage and saving for the future. It is only possible to evaluate these functions correctly when they are separated this way.

Whole Life, Universal Life, Variable Life, and Your Life

Now at long last we are going to perform this separation and look at the possible savings function of traditional life insurance. Because this work has a repeatedly stated bias in favor of not mixing the risk and savings components of a program (mainly because such mixing makes evaluation nearly impossible), you may guess in advance that only a few programs will appear attractive. Therefore, on behalf of the insurance profession and the many fine people involved in it, we are now going to take time out for a few kind words.

It will develop that you can probably get a better return from a tax-free bond fund than you can from even the best universal-life policy. But the bond-fund managers won't call up and nag you about paying your premium. The bond fund won't absolutely insist, with threat of stunning penalties, that you kick in $1,000 year after year whether you feel like it or not. So one way to look at traditional life insurance is as a psychological rather than a strictly financial institution. It creates a need to make regular savings deposits beyond the strivings of your own conscience.

There is not much point in making comparisons among different kinds of investments if it turns out that you are too lazy to make them. Thus you must evaluate this aspect of your personality before concluding that standard life-insurance policies are not for you. There are many, many families in the U.S. that are better off for having taken out a whole-life policy and keeping up the payments, however unfavorably such a policy may compare to more sophisticated self-directed investments. Keep in mind, however, that this kind of "hired will power" doesn't come cheap. We will present a review of the three main types of insurance and a table of representative cash values and compare this to the cash value you could expect from an alternative investment.

Whole life is the life-insurance policy that is most familiar. It is characterized by a large starting commission (usually at least 50% of the first year's premium) and by investment of your cash in the insurance company's general fund. Because the typical large insurance company is stuck with lots of long-term, low-yielding investments from the 1960s or earlier, the return is miserable by current standards. To make life insurance more attractive, many firms in the early 1980s began offering a variant called *universal life,* in which the cash balance is invested in money-market certificates. The linkage to traditional insurance is twofold: first, there is usually a commission (which may be smaller than for whole life), and second, the insurance company decides what your cash balance is (it does its own computation of the risk component).

Yet another variant is *variable life,* in which the investment component is a stock-market fund managed by the insurance company, often with the provision that the funds can be switched out to a money-market fund if the stock market goes sour. A further point to bear in mind about these policies is that they generally have a gruesome wipe-out provision if you lapse your payments. You can pay in $2,000 in the first year and then lose it all by letting your payments lapse at the beginning of the second. Look at this section of any policy carefully; about one-fourth of the policies currently being issued lapse in the first two years.

Program 7E will give as a result the amount of cash-value you would have accumulated after a number of years if there were no sales charges or internal costs associated with the insurance. The amount to enter as "annual premium" is the amount you are asked to pay beyond pure term insurance cost (this figure is available from Program 7B). We will take the case of a $100,000 policy as an example; for a male, age 35, the pure term-insurance component would be about $120. For the sake of argument, we will round this upward to $200 to cover insurance-company costs. The price of a typical whole-life policy with this benefit level would be $2,000 per year. This should leave $1,800 left over for the insurance company to invest on your behalf, right?

That's how it works in principle, at any rate. The program gives back the cash value for a given rate of investment return, and the idea is to try different rates until you find one that gives the same cash value as stated in the insurance policy. These days it is rather difficult to get the cash value information for some of the newer variable and universal life policies. Because these may depend on the performance of money-market funds in the case of universal life and the stock market for variable life, the policy may not have a neat little cash-value table as traditional whole-life policies do. Nonetheless, the performance of the policies over the last five to ten years is usually available.

Here is the program, followed by a typical application.

PROGRAM 7E
Cash Value

```
 50 PRINT "ANNUAL PREMIUM"
 75 INPUT P
100 PRINT P
125 PRINT "RATE"
150 INPUT R
175 PRINT R
200 PRINT "YEARS"
225 INPUT Y
250 PRINT Y
300 P=P/4
350 R=1+R/400
400 T=0
450 L=4*Y
500 FOR K=1 TO L
550 T=T*R+P
600 NEXT K
700 PRINT "CASH VALUE"
800 PRINT "=$";T
```

Table 7C shows what would have happened to the $1,800 savings part of the $2,000-per-year premium paid by our prototype 35-year-old male. Please keep in mind that most IRAs, which not by coincidence also will take a $2,000 contribution, would typically pay the highest yield listed in this table.

Table 7C Results of Program 7E for 35-year-old Male Paying Premium of $2,000 per Year

Effective Yield	Cash Value after Ten Years
3%	$20,901
5%	$23,170
8%	$27,181
11%	$32,071

(The program has assumed quarterly compounding; that's what's going on in lines 300 and 350.)

The situation in whole life is that ten-year cash values to compare to the numbers above range from $19,000 to about

$25,000 for the best yielding policies. It is easily possible to find policies in which, as an "investment," the interest rate is slightly negative. This happens because the sales charges and commissions can exceed possible interest earnings for the first part of the policy duration.

Another point to observe if you have limited funds available for investing is that money contributed to an IRA is tax-deductible, whereas insurance premiums are not. The interest earned in the life-insurance arrangement is tax-free (as, of course, is the interest in the IRA). This tax break on interest earnings used to be a major attraction of insurance. It still might be, if you have phenomenal amounts of money to salt away, but in practice you are unlikely to find an insurance program that pays as well as a municipal bond fund, which also offers tax-free interest.

The best universal-life and variable-life plans, which must usually be evaluated for five-year terms because they haven't been around that long, do much better on overall yield. What you will find if you collect some literature from the insurance firms is that the absolute best plans pay within a few percent of the best money-market rates, when commissions and other charges are taken into account. Although you might do better in a tax-free bond fund (some of these have no charges and offer free check-writing on the balance), you might like the feature that the insurance company will nag you about your premium payments; at least in this case the price you pay for artificial will power is minimal compared to the whole-life case.

A Summary for People Who Hate to Think About Insurance and Aren't Really Too Keen on Programming Either

The thing to do in health insurance is to take policies with the largest deductible you can stand. One thing you might consider doing is taking out a credit card, for example, VISA or Mastercard, that you consider to be an insurance card and leave in a desk drawer most of the time. Most hospitals (or auto body shops, considering car insurance as a similar example) take credit cards these days, and if you did get stuck with a large bill that you couldn't cover immediately you could just charge it and work it down later. This would still be a great deal cheaper than paying on a policy with a tiny deductible and correspondingly larger premiums.

For life insurance, first shop around for the cheapest term-life policy that will provide the amount of coverage you need. Then look at the amount of money you have left over for a savings plan. If you have just enough to fill an IRA for the year, or less, you probably don't have to consider insurance any further. If you find you have several thousand more dollars to stash somewhere, you might want to consider getting some literature on universal- and variable-life policies (the standard recommendation is a company called USAA Life in San Antonio, Texas, but many companies have improved their offerings in the last few years). Unless you have a strange condition, such as an estate worth more than $600.000, you most likely needn't bother with whole life.

The main point is to evaluate these policies by the numbers, without a salesman present. Even now there is a tendency for companies to make it hard to determine the relative amount of your money going into risk protection and into investment. Insurance is wonderful stuff, but there is little need to make extra contributions to some already very wealthy insurers.

8
Real Estate

The problem with real estate is that you are in the game whether you like it or not. You may refuse to keep a bank deposit, scoff at life insurance, and keep out of the stock market altogether. Presumably, however, you need some place to live and are either buying or renting. (This excepts those hardy souls in abandoned warehouses or the remote forests of the Northwest; they are assumed to read Thoreau exclusively rather than books like this one.) Thus you will need to consider these matters carefully, as the fraction of personal income spent on housing is now notably greater than it was even five years ago. This is a serious business, and there are right moves and wrong moves.

A Guaranteed, Safe Investment, Unless . . .

Here is the standard advice. Real estate is your best hedge against inflation. You just can't miss in real estate. Real estate is warmth, security, and motherhood. Get yourself some real estate and everything will work out fine. It should be no problem for you to walk into a bookstore and find a dozen books that tell you how to ". . . become a millionaire through real estate, with no money down, no brains, and no energy!"

Here is another side of things. One of the authors knows a hard-working couple in San Francisco (cat, parakeet, no kids, good education, Chardonnay, BMW, etc.). The fellow was making $38,000 per year at a large and well-known firm and his wife was earning $29,000 per year as a middle manager at the phone company. Realizing that their rent money was simply going down the drain, they decided to take the plunge and

buy a moderately nice "2Br/2Ba Sngl. fm. home" for $160,000,
at 7% down and 11% financing. So far so good. You will note
that the house is ridiculously expensive by middle-of-the-coun-
try standards; don't worry, as this story will turn out to have
Universal Significance.

The catch turned out to be that the young gentleman's
firm promoted him to its New York office. That was no problem
for these ambitious folks, who were in fact eager for challenges.
But in the intervening year, the standard rate for home loans
had risen to 15%. This meant that two things were possible:
either they would find a buyer for their house who would be
willing to carry much higher payments than theirs, or else
they would unload it at a much lower price to people who
could afford only the same monthlies that the current upscales
were accustomed to lugging. Let's look at the numbers. Here
is the situation for John and Mary Affordable, the original
owners.

Price	$160,000
Down Pmt	$11,000
Monthly	$1,420

And here are two classes of potential buyers, the Livewires,
who are not afraid of anything, and the Monats, who are trying
to keep their payments at the level the Affordables are paying.

	Livewires	Monats
Price	$160,000	$120,000
Down Pmt	$11,000	$8,000
Monthly	$1,880	$1,420

(These numbers have been rounded off slightly for
simplicity.)

The point of this exercise is that there are a lot more
Monats out there to go traipsing through your living room
on a Sunday-afternoon open house than there are Livewires.
This is not simply a matter of speculation; you can go look
up the statistical distribution of incomes from government tables. Not very many people can still buy groceries after mailing
$1,880 to the bank every month.

Guess what happened? They didn't get clobbered as badly
as they might have, not by a long shot. They found some people
who could take slightly higher payments and who for reasons

that are fairly neatly confuted by this very case, were optimistic about real-estate prices. These buyers closed the deal at $144,000.

Somebody lost $16,000 on this deal (that's $16,000 in one year, just to make sure that we all get the picture of how serious this is) and you may confidently bet that it wasn't the bank. Thus, the Affordables set off for New York with their $11,000 down payment wiped out to zero and $5,000 worth of personal debt.

Welcome to Vegas, High Roller!

Please recall, in the chapter on stocks and so forth, the particularly ill-natured jeremiad the authors set out on "margin trading" in general. Margin trading in stocks or commodities means making a down payment on the full price of a contract but taking the whole price change. *There is no brokerage firm in the world that would let you make the kind of gamble that expensive real estate represents.* A margin account at a commodity broker typically requires a large deposit to back up your losses, as a guarantee in advance that you have the resources to stand a loss. Yet, the most grandmotherly savings and loan will let you get in on a 10% margin deal on a hundred-thousand-dollar investment without batting a grandmotherly eyelash, and this situation is considered prudence itself. Of course, the reflexes of everyone involved in these transactions have been conditioned by decades of stable interest rates and conservative rules-of-thumb relating your income to the house you could afford. These reflexes are now dangerously slow and trusting.

The problem is that the price of a house cannot now be reliably counted on to drift steadily upward, but is critically linked to the cost of loan money. This cost now depends on many factors, some of which are beyond the direct control even of the government, and none of which have originated with events in your own neighborhood, however much they may impact the price of the house across the street. Consider Figure 8A, which shows interest indices for the period from 1979 to 1983.

If you buy a house, and particularly if you buy a house not to live in but to rent as a property investment, you are

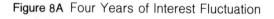

Figure 8A Four Years of Interest Fluctuation

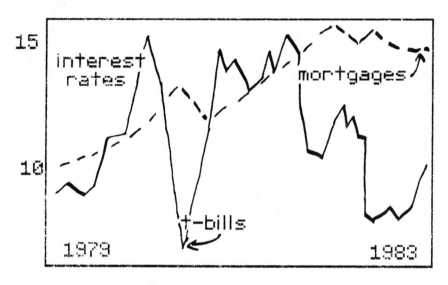

betting that you will be able to call the direction of these curves. Although many other factors affect successful real-estate investing, and let's hope you are very good at those factors, it is entirely possible to lose huge sums of money because of a six-month to one-year glitch in interest rates. This melancholy conclusion is one of the first points we wish to raise in this chapter, specifically because it seems to us that it is a feature of the market of the late 1980s that has been glossed over in many earlier real-estate books. Of course, it is possible to do well in this business, and we propose to present some programs and other information to assist you in doing just that. But please keep in mind that this is a trickier area than it was in previous decades.

Regionalism

You may try to console yourself with the thought that this particular problem is a California disease or a New York disease. This turns out not to be the case, and the reason is that value in real estate is driven by expectation. When interest rates are going up, it is clear that investors will have a harder time getting a higher price for properties. Likewise, when interest rates are going down, new speculations become possible. Recent data from the Federal Home Loan Bank have shown that a 1% increase in the average mortgage rate has had the effect of driving house prices down by 8% to 9%, in the short run at least. These, by the way, are average house prices throughout the nation, not the prices for isolated hot spots.

Nationally, there is reason to believe that real-estate prices in different regions are adhering to the same sort of pattern that we suggested in the stock market. In this pattern there would be four classes of city (actually the same analysis holds for farmland, if you wish to press the issue). Class 1 consists of cities with the cheapest house prices, for structural and industrial reasons. Prices in these cities tend to go up more slowly than the inflation rate in general; a good example in the last ten years is Detroit. Class 2 comprises cities with below-average prices but sound regional economies. Prices in these cities have tended to rise faster than the national real-estate indices. San Antonio, Memphis, and Atlanta are currently in this class. Class-3 cities, such as Washington, D.C. and Houston, are those in which the prices are above average and the rate of increase has slowed down. Class-4 cities are those in which real-estate inflation has outpaced the ability of the regional economy to support it. Examples in the mid-1980s are Los Angeles and San Diego; the prices in these areas are high enough to discourage practically anything except internal house-trading.

There is no doubt that in Class-4 regions every upward fluctuation in mortgage rates crowds out a great number of possible buyers. In California, a particularly bad example, a home-loan rate of 10% means that 18% of the families in the state can afford the average house (that's not especially wonderful, when you consider the other 82% of the families). A loan rate of 16% leaves only 6% of all families still in contention. And, mind you, we're talking about the average house. If you are trying, in a 16% mortgage market, to sell the fanciest house on the block—a little beauty with genuine marble bathrooms and a price about 50% higher than the house on either side—you are going to either wait a long time to sell it or take a real bath, so to speak, in all that marble. This linkage of rates to affordability tends also to be true even in cities with kindlier real-estate markets; in every area, people have a certain amount of resistance to paying much more than they expect for housing.

Hope

The preceding material, we hope, is gloomy enough to prevent anyone from approaching the rest of this chapter with dollar signs merrily twinkling in his or her eyes. There is plenty of reason for optimism about real estate as a long-term investment, however, assuming that we are not all blasted to eternity together by an international misunderstanding (in which case title insurance becomes equivocal). The reason that owning your own house is a good idea is that it provides almost the only necessity that is a major income-tax deduction. Most people know this already.

There are at least three good reasons for owning property that you intend to rent out. First, you can get long-term capital gains in real estate, giving you the same wonderful tax treatment on profits as you get with long-term capital gains in stocks. Second, while you are waiting around for your long-term capital gains, you get an immediate tax break in the form of a depreciation write-off. Third, unless you have an area of intense expertise, you can research your own local real-estate market more effectively than you can pick fast-track stocks; lots of people who don't know a CMOS RAM from a monoclonal antibody can tell when a toilet is leaking or a roof needs repairs. Note that none of these points touches on the question of profit from the rent itself. In many cases the tax breaks in real estate are sufficient to make people happy. We will look, however, into arguments against going into this for tax advantages alone.

The topics for the rest of the chapter will be owning your own home, renting, and holding property for resale. This will involve, ultimately, some longer programs, but these will be built up from small modules. When you get this program library assembled, you will find that you can compute your way to some straight answers on matters upon which real-estate agents are often, for reasons of their own, somewhat confusing.

Buying It

One of the core elements of any real-estate program is the section that computes mortgage payments from the mortgage amount and interest rate. Program 8A is a simple version of such a program; it assumes thirty years as the mortgage term (that's 360 months in line 230—change it if you must), and it departs from our usual line-number convention because it will end up embedded in a larger program. You can't have a real estate chapter without a mortgage calculator, so here is ours:

PROGRAM 8A
Mortgage Payments

```
200  PRINT "MORT AMT = "
205  INPUT M
210  PRINT M
215  PRINT "RATE = "
220  INPUT R
225  PRINT R
230  N=360
235  R=R/1200
240  P=M*R/(1-(1+R)↑(-N))
245  Q=12*P
250  PRINT "PMT = $";P;" YR = $";Q
```

Try this on a typical St. Louis mortgage ($40,000) and on a typical Silicon Valley mortgage ($160,000), at 12% in both cases. You should get payments of $411 in the Midwest and payments of $1,645 on the West Coast, explaining immediately why McDonnell-Douglas Automation Systems in St. Louis has a relatively easy time recruiting new computer-science graduates, while equivalent businesses in the homeland of the microcomputer have an uphill struggle. In fact, you may wonder how longstanding dreams such as home-purchasing are faring in more expensive areas; to see how people manage in the face of hideous economic adversity, we will have to add the next program section, which computes the tax break that comes from deducting mortgage interest payments.

Just enter Program 8B, with the earlier section (8A) still in memory. This new part gives a good approximation of the tax tables for 1984 and beyond. Type it in, and then we will explain the various features.

PROGRAM 8B
Tax Subroutine

```
110 A=2550
120 B=5270
130 C=1.25
140 Z=20000
150 F=1

800 I=I/F
820 Y=(I−Z)/Z
840 T=A+B*Y↑C
860 T=T*F
880 RETURN
```

Don't try to run this as it stands now; we haven't yet put in the section that calls for your income as an input, so you would get an error message from most BASICs. The 100-number part sets some constants for the tax computation. These particular numbers give the results for "Married, filing joint return." The numbers for other cases, that is, single, head of household, married filing separately, will be put in a section at the end of this chapter. Also to be explained later is the mysterious factor *F*. This is going to be a term that performs the currently mandated adjustment for Consumer Price Index changes; supposedly, this indexing will prevent bracket creep.

Now we will stick in the section that applies the tax computation to the case of your own home loan. With the 100-, 200-, and 800-number sections in memory, save them all to tape or disk under the name CORE or something similar. The two main programs on real estate will be just this core with different sections added. With CORE in memory, type in Program 8C.

PROGRAM 8C
After-tax Mortgage

```
300 PRINT "TAXABLE INCOME ="
305 INPUT I
310 PRINT I
315 GOSUB 800
320 V=T
```

```
325 I=I-Q
330 GOSUB 800
335 H=V-T
340 PRINT "TAX BREAK = $";H
345 L=(Q-H)/12
350 PRINT "EFF PMT = $";L
780 STOP
```

The program now figures your mortgage payments and then takes the payment total for the year to compute the reduction in your tax burden. The assumption in this simple version of the calculation is that all of the mortgage payments are going only for interest. This is certainly true for the first year of a new thirty-year mortgage and is close enough to correct for the first five years; because we are trying to get a guide to decisions you will make right now, this will be sufficient (the correction to take into account principal vs. interest parts of a mortgage is not difficult, but we are trying to keep things short).

Let us observe the effect of tax considerations on the St. Louis vs. Sunnyvale problem. The "effective payment" in the St. Louis case, for a taxable income of $50,000 per year (we are discussing upscale young joint-return moderns here, folks) is about $265 per month. For the same income level, the effective payments on the $160,000 mortgage are $1,107 per month. This is still not discount housing, but it is certainly an improvement over the $1,645 originally calculated.

As the income level floats higher and higher into the stratosphere, the effect of the tax deductibility of interest is to reduce mortgage payments by almost 50%. This is effectively a government subsidy; it amounts to letting people keep money that otherwise would be sacrificed to the federal budget deficit. Also, it should not be taken as wild encouragement to seek expensive housing. After all, deductibility is only a kind of discount— the people with the large mortgage are still paying 65 cents on every mortgage dollar after taxes, in this case.

Leaving these boringly prosperous characters for the moment, we shall run the program for a situation very close to the national median. Use $68,000 as the mortgage price (the median $78,000 house, circa late 1984, after a $10,000 down payment), 13% as the mortgage rate, and $29,500 as the joint taxable income. This income is a few thousand above the national family-of-four median but several thousand below the median for first-time home buyers. This produces monthly payments of $752 per month, and after-tax effective payments of $583. If you are renting at the moment and thinking of buying something, it is this last figure you should use in deciding what sort of payments you could stand if you set out to buy something. One thing you might consider doing, as an aid in house-hunting, is to make up a table of your effective payments for different mortgage amounts in advance; although there are many fine real-estate agents in this world, there are also any number who talk as if payments are nearly free "when you consider deductibility."

As a brief course in economic consciousness-raising, run the program above for 10% as a mortgage interest rate; this should give you payments of $454 per month instead of $583. That's a big difference. It is the main reason that banks and savings and loans all want to offer variable-rate mortgages. There is just no way these institutions are going to countenance letting you have a fixed-rate 10% mortgage if they feel the rates are increasing. They do, on the other hand, have a refreshing willingness to consider fixed-rate deals when rates are at historic highs. They can hardly be blamed for this; they, like you, are suffering the consequences of living in a country in which political understanding of economics is minimal. You as a potential homebuyer may often find yourself on the business end of government economic policies that are arguably described as punitive.

If your income is too low or too high, you may get an error message from the program. In this case consult the little appendix to this chapter for our recommendation. The approximation used to generate the tax level has been designed to fit only over a certain range; this is in contrast to the programs of chapters 4 and 9, which do the tax computation directly from government tables. Because in real estate we are mostly concerned with whether you can afford something or not, or whether a deal is favorable or not, the much simpler program here will serve our purposes quite nicely.

If you were to plot, for your income, the rent-vs.-buy price for a large range of mortgages, you would find some reinforcement for the argument for caution presented earlier in this chapter. In the more reasonable markets (Classes 1 and 2 in our scheme), after-tax mortgage payments tend to be lower than the rental of the equivalent property. This makes real estate a good investment for several reasons; one of them is the tendency of prices in these areas to catch up to the national averages.

The situation in class 3 and class 4 cities is quite the opposite. In San Francisco, a notoriously bad example, it is not difficult to find flats that rent for $800 that would call for a $140,000 mortgage if sold. For a couple bringing in $40,000 per year, the effective payments, even after taxes, would be $1,200 or so per month at 14%. Buying this property amounts to a bet that the high price levels will go even higher; it may happen, but the real-estate history of the U.S. contains the stories of hundreds of thousands of people who have been on the wrong end of bets like that. Such a flat may be a great investment for the owners who bought it thirty years earlier for $35,000 (their mortgage is likely paid off by now), but it is not necessarily a good investment for anyone at its current price.

So, if you're thinking about real estate, sit down with the computer and the want-ads on a Sunday afternoon and do some mathematical house-hunting indoors. Even the simplest situations can contain remarkable surprises.

Renting It Out

This next section will present a program that will give you your first year's return as a landlord. The program is a warm-up for one to be given later that includes selling the rental property, but it produces plenty of fascination in its own right. Call up the CORE program (100,200,800) and add this part.

PROGRAM 8D
Rental Return

```
400 PRINT "BLDG VALUE =?"
405 INPUT W
415 PRINT "MONTHLY RENT =?"
420 INPUT U
430 PRINT "ANN CASH EXP =?"
435 INPUT X
445 PRINT "TAXABLE INCOME =?"
```

```
450 INPUT I
460 GOSUB 800
465 V=T
470 I=I−W/18+12∗(U−P)−X
475 GOSUB 800
480 H=V−T
485 PRINT "TAX BREAK =$";H
490 E=12∗(U−P)−X+H
495 PRINT "NET RTRN PER YEAR =$";E
780 STOP
```

There are two ways to work this on your computer. First, you can simply delete the 300 block and have two programs stored on tape or disk, one for straight mortgage and one for rental. Second, you can put all the program in memory at once and add "jumpers" to steer the program to the right section; this means putting in

```
290 GOTO 400
```

when you want the rental section and putting in

```
390 GOTO 780
```

and removing line 290 if you just want the mortgage section. The choice is a matter of convenience. Our prejudice is always in favor of simplicity, so we recommend storing all this as two separate programs.

There are a few assumptions here that we should make explicit. In line 455 we are taking eighteen-year straight-line depreciation on the building. The government allows you to write off $\frac{1}{18}$ of the value of the building as a tax-deductible loss, every year for the first eighteen years you own the building (as of 1984). There is another method, called *accelerated depreciation,* that allows you to get bigger write-offs in the first few years and smaller ones later; we are sticking with straight-line here for simplicity. Also note that this is one of the sections of the tax code that attracts the most tinkering. Changes in these rules are proposed constantly. One of the most popular would be to change the depreciation period to twenty or twenty-five years (it used to be fifteen), which would result in smaller write-offs and thus more tax revenues. There is a grotesque federal budget deficit rumbling around out there, and you may be sure that there will be attempts to fix this situation in the dark alleys of the tax laws.

The building value to enter in this program is the property value minus the estimated value of the land. The building itself is regarded, in a way, as a piece of machinery that is wearing out, whereas the land is assumed not to depreciate. Occasionally, land ends up under the Mississippi or sliding into the Pacific, but these newsworthy events are presumed to be exceptions. The number you enter for building value will probably be about 80% of the number for mortgage amount.

Let's try an example. Take $200,000 as the mortgage amount, a 10% interest rate, building value of $160,000, $1,000-per-month rent, $2,500-per-year cash outlay (property tax, repairs, etc.), and a taxable income, for the lucky couple that owns this baronial fief, of $50,000. The first thing you are going to see is that mortgage payments are $1,755, so the $1,000-per-month rent is going to represent a large pre-tax loss. After the smoke clears over their Form 1040, however, their net loss for the year is seen to be about $4,905, closer to $400 per month than to the $900 it looked as though they were losing. This computation is not taking into account property taxes on the building or repairs, so in fact they will do slightly worse than this, but the program gives useful enough data; you can adapt this to your local situation by throwing in estimated taxes (remember that the taxes are reduced by your bracket percent).

Why, you inquire, would anyone mess with such an ostensibly unfavorable situation? (Perhaps you don't talk like that, but it's a good style for rhetorical questions.) The reason, and we will see later in detail how this works, is that if they can resell the building more than six months later at a profit they will be taxed at the long-term capital-gains rate. If the building can be unloaded with a $230,000 mortgage in two years, they will have made an astonishing amount of money. The building is then, of course, passed on to the next owners, who also lose money on the rent but hope to make it back in real-estate inflation, and so goes the merry chase. That is, until the market crashes, or "hiccups," or slumps, or "goes soft," or "cools off," or any number of things that aren't supposed to happen and are usually described as "only temporary."

But before we consider the amazing profits to be made in a rising market or the alarming tragedies that are possible when the market falls, we will look at a few details of the rental business.

Interest rates—10% vs. 14% The previous example showed our investors to be losing $4,905 per year at the $1,000-per-month rental level (this is the sort of thing that gives landlords a burning urge to raise the rent by a few hundred bucks). Consider, on the other hand, the situation when the prevailing interest rate is 14%. This produces a net yearly loss of $10,517. A little arithmetic shows that if they now wanted to break even on the rent they would have to raise it by $900 or so.

This has profound social consequences. It means that, when a building is sold that hasn't been on the market for twenty years, the rents are going to go through the roof. The old mortgage on the building we are discussing could have been for $50,000 at 6%; when the new paperwork is run up for $200,000 at 14%, the rents will simply explode. This is not an example of insatiable landlord greed (although examples of such are not unknown). It is a function of the real estate inflation of the last twenty years coupled with higher prevailing interest rates. When you see a newspaper story about some dear old folks being kicked out of the apartment they have been renting for twenty-five years, there are more villains than just the new owners.

As a practical matter, interest rates can change faster than listed real estate prices. If you are planning to buy rental property, you should run up a table for your own information showing net return for different building prices at different interest rates. You will rapidly convince yourself that it is advisable to wait out periods of high interest rates until either a) the prices of rental properties droop (this can take many months), or b) the interest rates come down. You will be in a much better position to figure your market timing if you have already formulated a table of possibilities.

The importance of location Just because you live in a particular town or city, it doesn't follow that there is any reason to buy rental property there. Your own home town may be, for example, ridiculously overpriced. The example cited above, of a $200,000 property renting for $1,000, is a real-life example from a large city that, for better or worse, adopted reasonably stringent rent control. Eighty miles outside of town, exactly that same amount of money will buy a "four-plex" that produces a total of $1,750 in rent. With the same parameters (income, building value, and cash outlay) and 10% financing, this property would return $1,390 per year. The rent takes care of the payments almost exactly, so the yield comes from tax savings. If the financing were done at 14%, the property would lose $3,734 per year, which is still fairly harmless compared to the big-city case.

A point that is sometimes overlooked is this: if somewhere within Saturday driving distance of your place there is a property that actually makes money (positive cash flow, as we say in the trade), why would you buy instead something else that loses money? Well, the answer is that you would be hoping for a big increase in the building price, but keep in mind that you are then planning to sell this to someone who would then lose even more money than you.

Two more points on behalf of positive cash flow are these (and, yes, we know it won't be easy to find these situations in some areas). First, if you find a place that is paying for itself, these days it means it is underpriced and is likely to make a larger profit upon sale. It also means that you will be able to wait for favorable market conditions without being hurried out by yearly losses. Second, if you are making a little money each month you are much more likely to be a good landlord. You will find it easier to order repairs and do regular maintenance; on simple grounds of availability of funds, plumbing repairs, for example, can be nearly impossible if a place is costing you $300 per month out of pocket already. We are trying to suggest that you are unlikely to have the proper spiritual attitude toward a building you are holding only for resale. So poke around through the ads for investment property using the program, and if you don't find a reasonable return, leave your money in a time deposit until things brighten up; remember, when interest rates are too high to make real estate a good buy, it is also the time you can get the best yield in a bank.

Visions of Sugarplums

All right. Look. Don't say we didn't warn you. All through this chapter we have droned on about reasons for caution. Lots of real estate is objectively overpriced these days. Prices do go down as well as up. Rapidly fluctuating interest rates make this business treacherous. And yet many people are furiously interested in investment property. We are about to explain why. Because this brings up the positively intoxicating subject of long-term capital gains, fasten your seat belts and avoid rich food before reading.

Recall our friends who have bought the rental property in the city, losing money at the rate of $2,605 per year. Suppose they unload the place after two years and clear $35,000 on the deal. This, by the way, is no great problem in a stable market; it only means that their property was inflating at roughly 8% per year, compounded. How much of this do they get to keep?

In the bracket in which these people are suffering, they would get to retain about $19,000 of the $35,000 if this were ordinary income. Because, however, it is a long-term capital gain, after depreciation recapture and accounting for two years of losses (!), they are left with $18,292 as the final return (we have neglected the appropriately negligible payments on the loan principal). Given that the investors in this case probably put about $20,000 down on the deal, they have made better than 90% return in two years. By the standards of anybody other than Brink's truck hijackers, that ain't too contemptible.

This can be summarized briefly. If you have found a property that is not already greatly overvalued, and if you can afford to hold onto it until inflation runs up its price by a reasonable amount, the tax laws of Our Republic guarantee that you will do very well indeed. Your profit will be taxed at 40% of your usual rate (this is the 1984 version of long-term capital gains and should hold for some time). Furthermore, you need to invest only the down-payment amount to take all the profit on a much larger sum. You thus obtain a truly wonderful return. At this point, you should add Program 8E to Program 8D and save the whole package.

PROGRAM 8E
Long-term Profits

```
500 PRINT "APPRECIATION (NET) =?"
505 INPUT S
510 PRINT S
515 PRINT "NMBR YRS HELD =?"
```

```
520 INPUT D
525 PRINT D
530 I=I+.4*(S+D*W/18)
535 GOSUB 800
540 PRINT "TAX ON SALE =";T-(V-H)
545 PRINT "OVERALL GAIN = $";S-(T-(V-H))+D*E
```

Line 530 contains the magic long-term capital-gains factor of 40%; if this were changed in the law to 50%, for example, you would just replace the 0.4 by 0.5. The number for "appreciation" asked for here is the check you would get from the escrow company, after all the parties involved have taken their commissions or fees. Recall that our hypothetical couple, with plenty of aid from the Internal Revenue Code and the double-edged razor known as leverage, was able to net a return of better than 90% in a two-year period. And this was from investing in property that sucked up the landlord's money like a tornado and appreciated at only about 11% per year. We will delve a bit more into the magic of taxes in this situation in the next chapter, but by now the point should already be clear. The profits would have been just about twice as abundant if the down payment had been only $10,000. This yield may be thought of as either "superior return on equity" or "obscene profiteering on basic needs," depending on whether you are the renter or the rentee.

There is a two-part dark side to this jolly show: personal and social. The personal dark side is that if you are forced to sell when the market is depressed you will get clobbered by the same miracle factor that produces the tremendous yield in better times. The social dark side is that all this "money-making" on inflation makes no one much better off. It's the same old building with a new price tag, and the correspondingly higher new rents probably just represent more transfer of funds from people who don't have large deposits to those who do (remember that the rent is going almost entirely to service bank interest on the mortgage). In this transaction, it could be said that you are earning a fee for improving the bank's loan position. Somebody has to own all this property, and we feel, dear reader, that it might as well be you, but it doesn't hurt to reflect sometimes that this is not the best of all possible fiscal worlds.

Appendix to Chapter 8

Here are tables for everyone else. Not everyone is married filing a joint return, of course. Substitute these sections for the different cases.

Single
```
110 A=1100
120 B=2020
130 Z=10000
140 C=1.333
150 F=1
```

This is designed for the income range $10,000 to $80,000.

Head of Household
```
110 A=1900
120 B=3860
130 Z=15000
140 C=1.25
150 F=1
```

This is designed for the income range $15,000 to $108,000.

The original program in the text, for married people filing a joint return, is designed for the income range $20,000 to $162,000. Outside this range there are fix-ups (you can put in a line that allows for incomes below the lower limit), but if you are serious you should wait until Chapter 9, wherein you will find the correct-to-the-dollar, table-based program.

If you are married but filing separately, you have probably noticed at some time that your tables are the joint tables divided by two. Thus your data set has A=1275, B=2635, and Z=10000.

The following routines concern indexing and inflation. These routines are the 1984 programs (for taxes payable in 1985). For subsequent years the tables are to be inflation-indexed, assuming they are not blown out altogether and replaced with a flat tax or some other novelty. A 6% increase in the CPI (Consumer Price Index) for 1984 would mean that F=1.06 would give the 1985 tables. The program scales back your income to constant 1984 dollars and then translates your tax into inflated dollars. For every year, there will be a correction factor F based on the CPI difference between 1984 and that particular year.

9
Tax Shelters

Attempting to cover the topic of tax shelters fully in a single chapter of a book is much like spending half an hour trying to harvest a forest full of lumber with a fingernail file. The best you could hope for is minimizing the damage to the crop.

Far be it from us to wreak havoc in a beautiful forest, so we won't try to bury you in all the clever concepts of the sophisticated shelters, much less insult your intelligence with the transparencies of some of the "shelters" that are prone to earn you shelter in a state-run institution for five-to-ten years. We *will* look at some of the general ideas common to all shelters, some simple ways to structure your day-to-day life to maximize the tax benefits, and the big gotcha in the "Alternative Minimum Tax" law.

Shelter is really in the eye of the deductor. We know a fellow we'll call Harry who makes a living doing tax returns but who suffers from a childhood dream of being a real, yippie-yi-yo, honest-to-Autry cowboy. Harry spent years deducting feed for his ranching clients and watching them make a profit on the sale of the herd the following year. After he purchased forty acres of wild pasture, he diligently prepared projections and analyses of his new beef-raising enterprise.

He calculated that he could make a $2,000–$3,000 profit if he raised five calves, which was the most that this plot of land could sustain without supplemental feed. He bought the calves in the fall, but the winter that year was rough. One of the calves died of pneumonia. Others needed veterinary care above and beyond the call of the budget. And the grass grew short, forcing Harry to purchase feed from the outside. He finally bailed out at a $3,000 loss during the summer.

Why relate this tale of economic woe in this chapter? Had Harry's ranch succeeded, he would have been able to tell his clients of his expertise in managing an enterprise, adding value to his financial counseling. As it turns out, he retrospectively calls his ranch a "tax shelter," adding credibility to his expertise as a tax wizard. Happily, Harry is an honest sort, who tells his tale in the same spirit that we do. He admits that it cost him more in out-of-pocket money than it saved him in taxes; this admission is the most unique part of the tale.

The moral here is that almost nobody at cocktail parties will ever admit to blatant failure in the investment world. If the loser doesn't boldly tell you that the whole idea was to save taxes, he will inevitably say something like, "Oh, well, I really needed the deductions." Keep this in mind when you reflect on the vast number of co-workers who seem to be involved with sheltering their income.

To the basics. A prior chapter defined taxable income as:

> Gross income
> − Some adjustments (for example, IRA deposits)
> − "Excess" itemized deductions
> − Exemption deductions
> _____
> = Taxable income

As mentioned, this covers only about 98% of the cases with which we're concerned. The other 2% will be ignored in the interest of sanity.

Anytime you doubt the validity of the following conclusions regarding changes in taxable income, you have verification tools at your command from Chapters 4 and 8.

In the past, we have referred repeatedly to tax brackets. Because a principal point we are trying to make is that it's far better to avoid focusing on the taxes, your authors have invented the phrase *net bracket*. It is defined as:

Net bracket = 1 − Tax bracket

If you are in a 28% tax bracket, then you're in a 72% net bracket. This enables us to put the focus on what's left, whenever it's appropriate.

Exemptions

Working backwards through these elements, *exemption deductions* become the first center of attention. In addition to being alive at some time during the taxable year, the only "shelter" the authors know intimately that uses this feature is having children. We have already emphasized the importance of looking at net-of-tax returns, rather than the amount of tax saved. Until the exemption deductions are significantly higher than the current $1,000 each, we cannot recommend large families as a viable way to come out ahead of the net-of-tax money game. You can also claim deductions for supporting in-laws and other panhandlers, but the economic consequences are similarly depressing. Of course, old age and blindness are qualifiers for these deductions, but these take patience and bad luck, respectively, to implement.

There is nonetheless a simple tip that focuses on exemption deductions. If several siblings are supporting Mom, who is a potential dependent, "multiple support agreements" must be filed. This is essentially an agreement as to which supporter among several will claim the deduction on his or her return. As long as no one supplies over half the support, *anyone* can claim the deduction, given that everybody agrees to the choice. It should almost always go to the supporter with the highest real tax bracket that year. The IRS has received a bit of a windfall from generous 50% taxpayers who let their 17% brethren take the deduction, on the theory that the destitute person has more need of the increased refund. Wrong. If you want to give money away to your friends or relatives, keep the deduction for yourself and give them hard cash. Giving them deductions while you get writer's cramp inserting the digits of your balance due only serves to give money to the government. Generosity and taxes don't mix well.

Itemized Deductions

Climbing up the basic outline of taxable income, we find that excess itemized deductions come into focus. Without meaning to sound redundant, we just can't emphasize enough the concept that *it is not worth going out of your way to spend money for the privilege of getting an itemized deduction.* Although this story could put a crimp in our credibility, we really have had someone—call her Sally—ask us whether she should take a Cal Vet mortgage on her new home at 9½% instead of a standard bank mortgage at 13%. After we determined that the interest rate charged was the only aspect that differed, we asked why she would even think of paying an extra 3½%, or about $2,000 a year, on a loan. Sally really thought that the loss of the $2,000 deduction could be more detrimental than the loss of the money. Of course, we did persuade her that the Cal Vet deal was by far the better choice; and, of course, we charged at the standard hourly consulting rate for this bit of financial genius.

The rule on interest payments is so simple that you can save electricity by turning your computer off and using the old noggin. Assuming that you're comparing alternatives that have the same degree of deductibility, you can simply *ignore taxes entirely when doing this comparison.* This is a simple tax truism that applies any time you compare two or more alternatives that have the same essential tax ramifications, and the only differences relate to actual dollars that move into or out of your pocket.

The Mortgage-interest Deduction

By the way, it seems that the deduction for interest on your home mortgage is reasonably safe, even under the proposed "flat-tax" changes. As we've mentioned, this is really the only necessity of life that can have a tax benefit attached, and it brings into question the motivations of those who insist on keeping this one in the law, while other deductions constantly suffer under the threat of annihilation.

Itemized deductions are theoretically those that Congress uses to promote "a better America." State taxes are deductible to be fair to those poor souls who live in expensive states. Charitable contributions are deductible to encourage donations to presumably worthy causes. Expenses of making more money (as discussed in Chapter 4) are deductible to inspire the country's gross national product (GNP) to new heights, increasing the tax base along the way. Home mortgage interest is deductible to—help those who can afford to be homeowners? Encourage more debt in America, an activity that is definitely not to the detriment of banks?

Actually, there was a time a few years back, during the Great Depression, when encouraging debt to stimulate banks and the housing industry made some sense. What are the social consequences today of this policy, which is so highly coveted?

At first glance, it would appear that housing would become more affordable; after all, the tax reductions associated with home ownership help pay for the shelter. But when you consider simple laws of demand and supply, making mortgage loans cheaper should increase the demand for them. When the demand goes up, the cost tends to rise, and the original "incentive" has been effectively removed by the mechanics of the marketplace. The cost of a loan is the interest you pay.

The graduated tax system, however, has changed one critical element. As we have pointed out, deductions are more beneficial to people in high tax brackets than to those at the lower end of the scale. The long-term effect of this break is that housing has become less expensive for high-bracket (rich) taxpayers and relatively more expensive for people in the middle and at the bottom. If this theory is valid, there would be finer homes for the wealthy, combined with an increasing number of people who can't afford to buy a home. Evidence for this abounds.

Why keep this deduction in lieu of others? We have found that most renters who are tossing pennies into a cookie jar (symbolically shaped like a house) actually want that deduction to stay around. They feel it's the one tax shelter that they themselves may someday be able to use. In other words, it's politically expedient; eliminating this deduction would be as popular as banning football games. Who said people know what's good for them?

Perhaps the biggest logical error these folks are making is a more sophisticated version of the same one made by Sally, with her choice of mortgages. They violate the tax-planning cardinal rule: *never focus on potential tax savings; keep your eye on what you're left with afterwards.* This applies to income as well as to deductions.

Beat the ZBA

One simple tip for those who have found they can almost itemize every year, but somehow just can't quite crawl over the
zero-bracket amount (ZBA). You can make the tax game more
like horseshoes, in which close is good enough. The trick is
to lump as many deductible payments as possible into one
year. If property taxes are payable in two installments annually, make an early payment, bunching three into this year,
and just one next year. Pay any anticipated balance due on
your state income taxes on December 31. If you've been ill,
and your medical expenses (including insurance) are more
than about 5% of your gross income, pay some premiums and
any other medical expenses you can get your hands on now.
If you attend church, when the plate is passed in December,
get generous; make up for it by being a tightwad next year.
Pay your accountant early. If you haven't yet read *Basic Money*,
buy it now. Next year, defer as many of these expenses as
possible.

    For example, if you're married, your total itemized deduc-
tions tally exactly $3,400 (the ZBA), and you have a couple
thousand dollars lying around, see if you can invest $1,000
or so in these expenses. They're all payments you'll eventually
have to fork over anyway. If you're in the 65% net bracket
(or 35% tax bracket), you'll save $350 in tax now. Next year
you'll spend $1,000 less and will be able to invest or enjoy
that money as you wish. Your itemized deductions will tally
only $2,400, but who cares? The government is going to charge
you exactly the same tax as if you'd had the $3,400. What we're
saying here is that this little technique yielded a safe net-of-
tax return of 35% in what amounts to less than one year—
for expenditures you would make anyway.

    The particularly astute reader may have noticed that we
seem to have violated our own cardinal rule here; we equated
the full benefit attained with the tax savings. This was a shortcut
born of experience and used here to test your alertness. The
trick here is that the analysis involved *only* expenditures that
would be made under any circumstances; the tax consequence
was the only aspect that changed.

    Try it the long way. Without juggling payment dates, a
total of $6,800 would be spent during the two years involved.
The effective deductible amount is zip, so the net misery is

the full $6,800. If some payments are moved into the first year, the same $6,800 is spent, but only $5,800 goes nowhere on the 1040 form; the deductible $1,000 really hurts you only at your net bracket, so only $650 of that $1,000 really comes out of your pocket. Total pain the second way is $5,800 + $650, or $6,450. This represents a savings of $350 over the unjuggled approach.

If you don't believe that careless use of the shortcut approach can be hazardous to your financial health, consider applying it to the popular offer to "Reduce Your Taxes! Contribute $1,000 to the League for the Preservation of Hairless Woolly Mammoths!" At a 35% tax bracket, you use the shortcut technique to conclude that you make $350 on this $1,000 out the door. The longer approach shows that you take $1,000 out of your pocket, but the cost to you at your 65% net bracket is only $650. This compares quite unfavorably with the alternative, which is to be plagued by greed and to keep the full $1,000 for yourself; cost to you is only a few passing guilt pangs for not helping the beasts in question. Your authors have spent many hours gaping at the effectiveness of "Need a tax deduction?" campaigns of charities.

Some Adjustments to Gross Income

Climbing farther up the basic outline of taxable income, we find that the next item is "some adjustments." This includes various deductions that Congress has decided should be deductible even for those who can't itemize. They include such non-shelter items as moving expenses, some employee business expenses, and the deduction for a working couple. IRA and Keogh plans are in here, but IRAs have been covered rather thoroughly already in Chapter 5.

Keogh plans are effectively pension plans available to self-employed folks and active partners in a business. For reasons somewhat too technical to delve into here, they are even better than IRA plans; and if you qualify for Keoghs, you can set up one of these along with an IRA. You can, that is, if you have a lot of spare change lying under the mattress.

Alimony falls into this category, also. The authors adamantly do not recommend that you go out of your way to establish a tax shelter that utilizes this deduction, but neither do we want to ignore it. Just in case you should happen to be among the computer enthusiasts who have sacrificed a spouse to your zealous ventures with silicon, you could wind up with a choice between alimony payments and child-support payments. The latter, at best, can result in a $1,000 deduction per child. This is undoubtedly less than you will actually spend on the payments. Alimony, on the other hand, is generally deductible in full, whether you can itemize or not; the payments are fully taxable as income to the recipient.

In an ideal divorce, the paying spouse will be instructed to write alimony checks if he (or she) is going to be in the higher bracket, and child-support payments if the bracket story is reversed. Similarly, in an ideal world, television raises the cultural level. Such ideals are achieved with roughly equal frequency. If you should happen to be on reasonably civil terms with your worthy opponent, use the tax-bracket calculator from Chapter 4 to your benefit (and the government's detriment). Enter the appropriate data statements from the single and/ or head-of-household tables. Then juggle potential interparty payments to try to put both people into the same tax bracket. If the total amounts you both agree to are more or less than the required amount, play with child-support payments and other considerations that have less direct impact on the tax liability. Under the 1984 tax law you can even stipulate in the divorce instrument that alimony payments be treated as non-alimony for tax purposes. Your attorney will be glad to help you in this creative divorce structuring—for a fee.

When he does, by the way, make sure that he states on his bills the charge for the time involved in structuring payments for tax purposes; that portion of the bill qualifies as an itemized deduction, although the rest of the divorce legal fee qualifies only as expensive.

The "gross income" part of the formula is where the major shelter battle tends to be waged. There are three basic ploys used here. All of them have already been introduced elsewhere in this book. One tack is to keep the income permanently out of this area entirely, either through nontaxable income or through deductions that will never come back to haunt you. Another is what we call *mañana money;* don't pay taxes today if you can hold off the taxability until tomorrow. Finally there is the magic of capital gains, which can give you 60% of your profit tax-free. When you combine these last two, it can only be described as alchemy—a true windfall if you use it, and an evil science if you envy those who do.

Note that we mentioned deductions. In *gross* income? The word *gross* here is quite deceptive. It includes *net* income (or loss) from self-employment, rental properties, farms, partnerships, and a few other things. The tax forms try to alleviate the problem by referring to it as "total income." The above explanation is still valid, and still warranted; total income isn't total (and there are times when you may be convinced that 1040 "income" isn't income).

GROSS-INCOME TRICK # 1
Keeping Earnings Out

Chapter 5 gives an example of keeping your hard-won earnings entirely out of gross income. When you earn interest income on municipal bonds or funds composed of these vehicles, the money deftly skirts the Form 1040, going straight into your pocket. From the investor's point of view, muni-bond interest is the principal source of nontaxable income. Others, such as Nobel prizes, are somewhat harder to implement.

Although many people include barter and "cash" income in this category, we must point out that this is a common deception. If you plan to invest your nest egg in a farm that specializes in a popular intoxicating cash crop, please be aware that you will have two reasons to avoid reporting this income. You may feel that evasion of tax is a favorable by-product of the other reason, but you should study the life and times of Al Capone. When the authorities couldn't pin any other raps on him, tax evasion was sufficient to enforce his move to Alcatraz.

One legitimate way to keep earnings on investments out of your gross income is to put it into someone else's gross income. Children tend to be prime targets, because most of them are in the 100% net bracket. An old ploy is the interest-free loan to the child, which he or she pays back after accumulating gobs of income without paying tax on it. In 1984 Congress lowered the boom on this one, though, and it has become a technique without a future. Still remaining are gimmicks such as Clifford trusts and outright gifts to minors.

Clifford trusts will be ignored here, because the readers of this book will generally find them to be primarily a good way to invest $2,000 in their attorney's bank accounts. Gifts

are another matter. Most states have enacted some form of
the Uniform Gifts to Minors Act (UGMA). The idea of this
act is to make it affordable for a couple or individual to make
a gift to a child, although the donor retains control over the
money until the youngster becomes an oldster, which is usually
deemed to be at the ripe old age of eighteen. Up to $10,000
may be given by each adult to each child each year without
their even having to file a gift tax return.

If those last three words aren't familiar to you, we'll be
glad to amuse you with the unexpected. Despite the teachings
of the Judeo-Christian ethic—'tis better to receive than to give—
it's the donor who must file the gift tax return and who bears
the responsibility of paying any gift tax. This is nothing new,
because the gift tax has been here far longer than the income
tax. Merry Christmas!

The advantage of a UGMA gift is that the first $1,000 in
income is completely free of tax. Unlike single adults, dependent minors get no ZBA on "unearned" income (that is, income
the minor doesn't have to work for), so the only deduction
they have is the $1,000 exemption for living. Then the income
crawls through the brackets, starting at 11%.

The disadvantage of a gift to a minor is that you really
do have to make a gift. You can't take the money out of the
UGMA account to pay the mortgage; the only allowed withdrawals are for the kid's necessary expenses. And if the child's
fiscal diligence remains that of a child when he or she turns
eighteen, that "college fund" could quickly take on the shape
of a metallic blue BMW. We therefore recommend this tax-
saving technique only to the incurably optimistic. After getting
this far in *Advanced Money*, we sincerely expect that there
are very few readers stranded in this category.

GROSS-INCOME TRICK #2
Mañana Money

The second major technique, mañana money, is based on the
premise that you would rather have a dollar today than a dollar
tomorrow. This is called "present value" by human number
crunchers. A program in *Basic Money*, which was ostensibly
about zero-coupon bonds, is really a calculator of present value.
It is reproduced here, in slightly modified form, as Program
9A.

PROGRAM 9A
A Buck in the Hand

```
100  PRINT "FUTURE VALUE = ?"
110  INPUT H
120  PRINT H
130  PRINT "DISCOUNT FACTOR =?"
140  INPUT R
150  PRINT R
160  PRINT "NUMBER OF YEARS =?"
170  INPUT L
180  PRINT L
190  P=H/(1+R/100)↑L
200  PRINT "PRES VAL = $";P
210  STOP
```

This little program will tell you the value of a promise (in the financial sense). As an example, suppose that someone has promised to fork over to you $2,000, and assume for now that you positively know that this person is true to her word. If the money is coming today, you can promptly figure out, without the aid of a computer, that the value of this promise is $2,000. But what if the money is coming a year from now? Run the program, using a future value of $2,000, a discount factor of 12, and a time span of one year. The discount factor, by the way, is basically the net earnings you think you could make on the money each year you had your greedy paws on it.

The calculated present value is $1,786, which, as anyone of moderate intelligence can readily determine, is somewhat less than the $2,000 stated amount. If you run the same future value and discount rate for a longer period, say five years, the present value drops to $1,135. Using one year again, but dropping the discount rate to 10%, the present value is $1,818, a bit more than in the first instance.

All of this makes intuitive sense. The longer the wait, the more time you lose, and the old saw about time and money applies here perfectly. A lower discount factor means that the time lost isn't as critical, so the present value wouldn't drop as much.

The beauty of this program is that you can now quantify these instincts, allowing you to make more rational decisions when the going gets more complicated. If one investment promises that you can bail out after ten years with $5,000 in your pocket, how does it compare to another opportunity that claims to give you $2,000 two years down the road? Run the numbers on your computer to discover that, at a discount factor of 12%, the $2,000 in two years is marginally better.

Save the program, and while the disk or tape is whirring, consider how this works in the tax-deferral environment. Think in terms of money leaving your pocket, which, of course, is exactly what taxes tend to do. In this light, a tax you pay tomorrow hurts less than one you pay today, as long as the money that is being taxed is still productive for you.

To handle this, bring up the CORE program from chapter 8. Now replace lines 200–250 with the exciting stuff in Program 9B.

PROGRAM 9B

A Tax in the Bush

```
200 PRINT "TAXABLE INCOME =?"
205 INPUT I
210 PRINT I
215 GOSUB 800
220 V=T
225 PRINT "AMOUNT DEFERRED =?"
230 INPUT D
235 PRINT D
240 PRINT "NUMBER OF YEARS =?"
245 INPUT L
250 PRINT L
255 PRINT "DISCOUNT FACTOR =?"
265 INPUT R
275 PRINT R
280 I=I+D
285 GOSUB 800
290 H=T−V
295 PRINT "ADD'L TAX = $";H
300 W=D−H
305 PRINT "WITHOUT DEFER. = $";W
310 P=H/(1+R/100)↑L
315 PRINT "PRES VAL TAX = $";P
320 PRINT "PRES VAL DEFER. = $";D−P
```

```
325 PRINT "BENEFIT = $";D—P—W
780 STOP
```

The approximate taxes calculated by the CORE program will be quite sufficient for this purpose. To start with an example of a "one-year" deferral, assume that you're married, it's 1984, and, in direct defiance of our earlier warnings, you've invested in Kosher Pork Belly Futures. Assume further that you've managed to strike it rich anyway, and you're sitting on $2,000 short-term gain on December 31. What's the tax cost of selling today, rather than waiting two days? At this time of year, two days is as good as a year for tax deferral; the two-day wait for the actual money is sufficiently minimal to ignore completely.

Given that you have $50,000 other taxable income and that you use a discount factor of 12%, the additional tax you would pay immediately by selling in December would be $735, meaning that you would keep only $1,265 of the $2,000 profit. Quantifying the virtue of patience for the two days, the present value of the tax due a year late is just $656. Because the deferral of the gain itself is negligible, you now net the equivalent of $1,344, a $79 improvement. This represents a 4% increase in your net-of-tax gain by waiting two days. It's worth it; think of all the additional computer books you could buy with an extra $79!

How about a longer deferral? Keep all the facts the same, except that this time, instead of a commodity gain, you have decided to put $2,000 into a deferred compensation plan that your employer has just set up. This money will be earning income (you hope) in your name, so you've effectively received the use of it today. But the taxes won't take the bite for, say, five years, when you pull it out. The program shows that the deferral is worth about $318 to your financial well-being, excluding the benefits of deferral on the income earned. Does this remind you in any way of an IRA?

Another twist on mañana money is that it works just as well for taking deductions now, even though these deductions show up as income sometime down the road. Using the same basic background, this time you've purchased a partnership interest in the "Right Off! Tax Shelter" limited partnership, which, among other things, elects to immediately deduct a computer that the partnership bought. Your share of this write-off is $2,000. If, by some fluke, the partnership is able to pawn it off at its original cost five years later, the $2,000 would come back to you as ordinary income. Economically, the deduction and the income are a wash—except for the timing. If you enter "−2000" for the amount deferred, the computer will tell you there is a negative benefit of $313. Because ignoring the sign is easier than modifying the program, take the lazy approach, fully realizing that this chunk of mañana money is worth $313.

GROSS-INCOME TRICK #3
Capital Gains

The third key element of sheltering income is the capital-gain benefit, which we've already discussed to some extent. But a little more detail can be remarkably profitable. There are times when mixing things together is to everyone's benefit. Wonderful examples include Waldorf Salads and Mu Shu Pork. Mixing long-term capital gains with short-term capital losses, however, is more like tossing a few gallons of oil into your radiator. It costs you.

As a result of the 1984 Tax Reform Act, you have to hold on to the item being sold for only six months and a day *if* you acquired it between June 23, 1984 and December 31, 1987. Other property has to be retained for more than a year to qualify.

There are a few basic rules in calculating capital gains and losses, and we'll express them as a BASIC program momentarily. In English (or at least as close to English as possible), net long-term gains receive very favorable tax treatment; generally only 40% is taxed. Net long-term losses, on the other hand, are unfavorable because you can deduct only 50% of the amount. Net short-term gains and losses are taxable and deductible, respectively, in full. In all cases, the maximum deduction allowed in any one year is limited to $3,000; any additional loss claimed may be carried forward to future years.

The rub in all of this lies in that recurring word *net*. First you are required to combine all long-term transactions with each other, coming up with a singular "long-term" amount. Then you do the same thing with short-term transactions. Finally, you combine the two numbers and tax what you've got.

Performing the combination in BASIC would be easier than doing it English. Delete lines 200–325 from the last program, then just pop in Program 9C.

PROGRAM 9C
Capital Gain and Loss Calculator

```
400 PRINT "TAXABLE INCOME =?"
405 INPUT I
410 PRINT I
415 GOSUB 800
420 V=T
425 PRINT "LONG-TERM +/− = ?"
430 INPUT L
435 PRINT L
440 PRINT "SHORT-TERM +/− = ?"
445 INPUT S
447 PRINT S
450 N=S+L
455 X=0
460 IF N<0 THEN GOTO 500
465 IF L<=0 THEN 480
470 X=L
475 IF N<L THEN X=N
480 D=.6*X
485 E=N−D
490 PRINT "NET TXBL GAIN = $";E
495 GOTO 550
500 IF S>=0 THEN E=.5*N
505 IF L>=0 THEN E=N
510 IF S<0 AND L<0 THEN E=S+.5*L
515 PRINT "NET TXBL LOSS = $";E
520 IF E>=−3000 THEN GOTO 550
525 PRINT "LIMITED TO $3000 FRST YR"
550 I=I+E
555 GOSUB 800
560 PRINT "TAX CHANGE = $";T−V
565 PRINT "NET AFTER TAX = $";N−T+V
570 PRINT "PERCENT YOURS =";100*(N−T+V)/N;"%"
```

You tally up the long and the short of it; the program does the rest. If the deductible loss exceeds $3,000, the program merrily goes along as though the whole thing is deductible in the current year, but it does give you a warning message. This will suit our purposes quite well.

It has already been shown that mañana money can give

Table 9A Capital Gain and Loss Insights

Go #	Long-term Gain/Loss	Shrt-term Gain/Loss	Net Txbl Gain/Loss	Net aftr Tax	Eff Net Bracket
1	$3,000	$ 0	$1,200	$2,560	85.3%
2	0	−3,000	−3,000	−1,920	64.0%
3	3,000	−3,000	0	0	N/A
4	−3,000	0	−1,500	−2,457	81.9%
5	0	3,000	3,000	1,893	63.1%
6	−3,000	3,000	0	0	N/A
7	3,000	3,000	4,200	4,443	74.1%
8	−3,000	−3,000	−4,500	−4,392	73.2%

you an after-tax profit even when you have a pre-tax break-even situation. Now it's time to show that capital gains can pull the same magic, if you handle them with care.

We've used this program to produce Table 9A, which summarizes various gain and loss situations. An analysis will yield some potentially bountiful morals. In all cases we've assumed a married couple with $50,000 in other taxable income in 1984; by now, this scenario should have become boringly familiar.

The first two runs show how to break even and let the government boost you into a profit. Long-term gains of $3,000 recognized in a single year net you $2,560; you keep 85.3% of the gain for your own use. As expected, only 40% of the gain, or $1,200, suffered the slings and arrows of the IRS. Short-term losses in the second round, when recognized without anything long-term going on, cost you only $1,920 of your own money, the other 36% being courtesy of the treasury. Combining these two, which normally represents a pre-tax no-win situation, we pocket $640 after all the smoke clears. Will miracles never cease?

Unfortunately they do cease all too often, as a result of one of the most common misunderstandings investors have. If you recognize both the loss and the gain in the same year, the third run through the program shows the bland consequences; the break-even is treated as though it were a break-even. *If you have long-term gains, do not strive to offset them with short-term losses in the same year.* Patience is a virtue here, as you can beat the game by using those losses to produce real tax savings in the following year.

The fourth run shows that only 50% of long-term losses serve to your benefit on the 1040. In the fifth run, short-term gains have all the thrilling benefits of ordinary income. If you combine these two events into the same year, however, the bottom line is the same as it was on the third run; if net gains and losses are zero, that's what the tax consequences are. Period.

Mentally combining runs 4 and 5, you can see that, although it appears that your investments have gone nowhere, the tax code sets you up for a ding anyway—you're behind $564 after this obnoxious income tax on no income! Putting both transactions into the same year, however, alleviates the damage. *Short-term gains are excellent vehicles for offsetting long-term losses.* Try to avoid naked long-term losses whenever possible.

The final two runs complete the display of the interaction between capital gains and losses. When both long and short positions are gains, you're hit with a tax on the full short-term gains plus 40% of the long-term. If both are losses, all of the short and half of the long-term losses are deductible, but, as we've noted, the maximum deduction is limited each year to $3,000.

Use this program to your benefit whenever you feel a need to see what wonders you can create for yourself as your gains and losses for the year are taking shape.

Mañana Money + Capital Gains = Alchemy

Now we can glance briefly back at rental investments and see what it is in the tax code which makes them so droolingly attractive—at least in terms of tax benefits. How about taking depreciation today, as an ordinary mañana-money move, but when it comes back to grab you, it returns as capital gains. Such use of two ploys at one time is clearly a form of alchemy, and it's a privilege accorded rental property by a most benevolent Congress. Never underestimate the determination of the real-estate lobbyists.

Toss in a pinch of volatility, which is added by leverage, and you have one outrageously stacked deck. We'll ignore present value on this for simplicity, but it's time to dig into the program archives to give the last program from chapter 8, Program 8E, one more trial. This one will isolate tax consequences. Assume a property purchased for $220,000, with $20,000 down. The mortgage amount would be $200,000; the interest rate is assumed to be 10%. In deference to tradition, we'll once again use the 1984 married couple with $50,000 in other taxable income. The building value is, once again, $160,000. In addition to the mortgage, cash-flow elements are $2,400 in annual expenses and $1,955.14 rent earned per month.

$1,955.14? If you run the program, you'll find that the monthly mortgage payments total $1,755.14. After considering that other cash expenses total $200 per month, this is about as close as you will ever come to a perfect pre-tax bore; cash out exactly equals cash in. Assume that, at the end of two years of ownership, this property has appreciated exactly enough to cover selling costs, so there is no real gain or loss on selling this building. Overall gain after tax goodies? $3,239, and every penny of this is straight from the treasury. This pathetically simple investment has returned over 16%, or 7.75% compounded annually, in a two-year period. Net of income tax—*because* of income tax! Before the 1984 Tax Reform Act extended the "life" of a building, the return would have been about 10.5% compounded annually.

Organized Tax Shelters

So far we've been concentrating on tax shelters you create yourself, but there are a lot of limited partnerships out there that will encourage you to save on taxes by casting your fate with them. On occasion, you may even get lucky and find one that's legitimate enough to emphasize prospective returns on the investment net of tax.

Most organized shelters, and many home-brewed ones, use aspects other than those buried in taxable income; *credits* against the tax have been rising in importance since the mid 1960s. The principal one you're likely to encounter in organized tax-shelter literature is *investment tax credit* (or just *investment*

credit), which basically gives a tax benefit to companies or
individuals purchasing equipment for such trades or businesses
as oil drilling and jojoba bean farms. Another is a credit for
performing research and development. We won't concern ourselves with the technicalities of these, but it might come in
handy to have some idea of how they can benefit you.

The difference between a credit and a deduction is both
simple and critical. As we have noted, a deduction reduces
taxable income and thus gives a benefit directly proportional
to the tax bracket:

$$\text{Benefit} = \text{Tax Bracket} * \text{Deduction}$$

A credit, on the other hand, cuts taxes dollar for dollar:

$$\text{Benefit} = \text{Credit}$$

Often in shelter literature you'll see enticing statements
such as "Total tax benefits, in the first year, equivalent to
\$_____ (enter an extravagant amount) in deductions." En-
ticing, but not terribly enlightening. To determine the "equivalent in deductions" of credits for your own circumstances, use:

$$\text{Deduction} = \text{Credit} / \text{Tax Bracket}$$

In other words, you need to know what tax bracket the pur-
veyors of the shelter assumed when they did their own calculations. Of course, you'll also see "Total tax benefits of
\$_____ (fill in one-half the amount you entered above)."
The two statements are equally useless. Know your own
bracket, then dive into the literature to find out how much is
from deductions and how much from credits. Then the programs in this book can be used to help you take a stab at
the benefits you can get from deductions; simply add the credits
to find your total tax break.

Once you've gotten this far, *do not stop*, unless you've
already decided to sacrifice the prospectus to the office shred-
der. Put things in perspective; it's not worth spending \$2,000
in real money to save \$1,000 in tax. If a salesman stops here,
let him find the door himself. The unavoidable question that
must be resolved is, "How much money will I make—net after
taxes—when it's over?"

The Lurking Peril: The Alternative Minimum Tax

Before leaving the topic of shelter, we must fulfill our promise to introduce you to the Alternative Minimum Tax (AMT). This is specifically designed to remove much of the glow from the good things in tax life.

In the late 1960s, a number of prominent people were filing returns with lots of income, lots of loopholes, and no tax. In 1969, Congress was finally pressured into recognizing this obscenity, which had infuriated almost everyone else. They put in a minimum tax, commonly called a "loophole" tax. It was something of a token gesture at first, but it has evolved into a legitimate threat.

We definitely don't want to explore details here. One of the authors recently attended a seminar at which he had the pleasure of observing fifteen or twenty accountants spend hours trying to figure out the AMT. The basic idea, however, is not that tough to understand.

Conceptually, everyone who files a tax return is required to pay the regular tax or the AMT, whichever is greater. As a practical matter, it usually applies only in cases in which certain loopholes, such as capital gains and investment tax credit, are used to substantially reduce the regular liability. The AMT has its own version of gross income, itemized deductions, exemption, preferences, and a tax table of sorts. Actually, the table is quite short—a flat rate of 20%. The exemption is $40,000 for married taxpayers and $30,000 for single. Sorry, but your kids don't bring you another dime in deductions here.

This may seem lenient, and you may almost wish that it applies to you. Don't get too enthusiastic. This comes into play only if it makes matters worse, never better. And there's no capital gain deduction, investment credit, accelerated depreciation, or dividend exclusion. Also, itemized deductions are highly restricted. In particular, state taxes and (dare we whisper it?) those miscellaneous expenses, such as accountants and this book, become nondeductible, and the only medical expense that will help the liability is the part that exceeds 10% of your gross income. There is a host of other deductions and credits that disappear when this tax is computed. The main point is that this "loophole" tax no longer hits only the very wealthy. It seems that a progressively larger sampling of the real world is being introduced abruptly to this beast.

The biggest problem is that it changes tax planning so substantially from one year to the next. For example, many of the deductions that flow through to partners in most of the organized tax shelters will be totally worthless to an AMT taxpayer; the wisdom of owning the shelter must be re-evaluated. And you should make the lowest legal payments for state income taxes during an AMT year. We know one fellow who, after being assaulted by accountants for thirty years with advice to make advance payments on his California taxes during big years, prepaid a large bit of change to his state tax board in December. He had just made a killing on some rental property that he'd held for twenty years. This was a capital gain of some $200,000. AMT reared its ugly form, and those state-tax checks can *never* be deducted. The resulting financial pain will hopefully subside someday.

Many accountants have mixed feelings about the AMT. They don't like hearing their clients whining, but the additional planning required with it has made the bill that put the AMT into law a veritable "Accountants' Full-Employment Act."

The main point is that if you should decide to start taking lots of advantage of some of these tax ploys, the AMT may strike. When it does, your whole tax world turns upside down.

While we're on a roll with warnings, we might as well toss in one or two more. Unless you're the sort who enjoys waiting for action in dark alleys, stay away from the extremely aggressive organized tax shelters. Rumor has it that the IRS is sending letters to some people saying, in effect, "If you claim any of the following deductions through Deductitall Investors, they will automatically be disallowed." This is not the least bit pleasant to discover after you've placed your bets.

Even if you stick to very "clean" partnership shelters, you can have problems. It's called too much of a good thing. We knew one fellow (George) whose income suddenly jumped from $30,000 per year to $180,000 per year. (Inheriting a company presidency can be invigorating!) He decided to get into some real-estate partnerships to protect this income. Alas, he was a real sucker for a salesman; he bought about 17 such partnership interests within two years. Because this was before the AMT came into being, he paid absolutely no tax. That's the good part. The bad part is that, despite this very reasonable income, he had to borrow money to buy groceries. Everything he earned went straight into the tax shelters. When the accelerated depreciation started decelerating, the interest-paid started to drop, and the rents charged started to rise, these shelters started producing taxable income of their own. Solution? More shelters. We don't know whether George ever escaped from this spiral, but we do know that he did it alone. His family of twenty years left him; the chaos was more than they could handle. Realistically he would have been better off just paying taxes full bore. And enjoying life.

A number of tools in the tax laws can be used to your benefit. After all, other people are using them. Because the theoretical *raison d'être* for these laws is that they're good for the country, you could consider it your patriotic duty to use them. But there are warnings we must issue: keep your eye on what you have left after taxes, don't get careless with your timing, be ready to change direction quickly, and don't get too greedy.

10
Scenarios

All the advice of the previous chapters is based on the assumption that the economic performance of the United States, its financial markets and stock market, will continue to fall within the performance ranges of the last twenty years. That is, we expect an inflation rate between 2% and 20%, with no substantial deflation, an unemployment rate between 3% and 15%, and interest rates between 6% and 20%. These ranges will be the definition of *normal*, and it will be pointed out that quite different investment strategies apply once things get outside these familiar conditions. At 12% interest, 3% inflation, and 3% unemployment, you would be happy to have lots of money in T-bills; at 120% inflation and 40% unemployment, you would be happy to have lots of Campbell's soup and a shotgun. In this chapter, we will take a look at the forces affecting these three terms in the economic equation and suggest a few computer models for interpreting their impact.

In developing a model of the next decade or so, we must take into account four features of current economics that appear unlikely to go away soon. These are monetary dislocation, government spending, energy problems, and technological advance. All these are in fact linked to one another, with energy and technology among the more obvious connections. Although this model may appear to require an attempt to see into the future, actually it will be an attempt to get as much prediction as possible with the minimum foresight.

The guide in these matters is an anecdote about Enrico Fermi, the brilliant Italian physicist who came to the United States before World War II and contributed the foundations of reactor development and the Manhattan Project during the war. In the late 1930s and early 1940s Fermi was still at Columbia, and he participated in an informal faculty group called the Prophet's Club. The members of this club would make sealed predictions about the events of this turbulent period; several months later they would open them and rate the predictions for accuracy. Apparently, Fermi almost invariably won these little contests. And he did so, typically, by predicting that not much would happen. The rate at which people imagine exciting events to occur almost always outstrips the rate at which they do occur; the consequences of major economic events can take decades to be felt completely.

Keep this in mind, if you will, as you peruse the books on economic topics that have been published in the last ten years. You will see that you are always being counselled about Surviving the Coming Crash, Profiting from the Coming Boom, The IRA as a Sure Thing, or Gold Coins in Your Backyard. Although the exact strategies for investing change considerably as interest and inflation rates go up and down, none of the conditions that have actually occurred has been beyond the "normal" range for which the investment strategies of this book are valid.

At the end of this chapter we will include some notes, for those who like a little excitement in their lives, on warning signals that might indicate that all bets are off and that things are hopelessly wrong. In the meanwhile, however, it is wiser and for that matter less notably antisocial to assume that you are going to have to soldier on under less-than-optimal but not disastrous conditions.

Four Major Problems

PROBLEM 1
Monetary Dislocation

Here is a crude summary of an important problem. For a long time after World War II, petroleum was extremely cheap in comparison to its importance in industrial economies. Then in 1974, OPEC succeeded in raising the price of oil rapidly and thus transferring a huge pile of cash from the industrial economies to the Near East. What happened to this cash, given that the relatively underpopulated oil states could not absorb it in their own economies? They put large amounts of it in short-term deposits in banks back in the industrial countries, particularly the dear old stable USA. The banks, suddenly awash in oceans of new dollars, proceeded to make a series of huge loans to countries in Latin America and Eastern Europe. The global economy then slumped, the price of oil went down, and a truly terrifying fraction of these giant loans are now for all practical purposes "nonperforming." The theory in these loans was that sovereign states do not default on their obligations. So far this has been true, at least technically, but it is also true that sovereign states have more ways of rearranging their payback schedules than you have. When your auto loan becomes "nonperforming," rest assured that your bank will see to it that you will be taking the bus to work very soon. When the same thing happens to Argentina, the debt gets "restructured" so that the bank can pretend that all is not lost. Powerful as Citibank is, it cannot seize Buenos Aires; in fact the power of Citibank, as you read this, may have been more forcefully applied in suggesting to the U.S. Congress that these loans should be protected indirectly by the American government.

This may have gone past you a bit rapidly, so we will recapitulate. You paid all this money to the oil companies, who sent it to OPEC, who sent it back to New York. The New York banks lent it to various South American countries, who spent it and can't pay it back. There is now an excellent chance that these same banks will get the government to bail out their bad loans, using your tax money. If you feel somehow that none of the principal participants in this merry chase has your interests at heart, you are probably right. The notorious lack of interest of the American voting public in most economic matters results in this same public having exactly no protection against organized multinational maneuvers.

Partly because the price of oil is still rather high by historic standards, and partly because the apparent immunity of the U.S. to serious political change makes it seem stable by the standards of much of the rest of the world (consider the nationalization of banks in Mexico or industry takeovers by the French government in the name of socialism—and these are hardly revolutionary states), there are still large deposits to be found at the major American banks. These deposits are very sensitive to the relative interest rate vs. inflation rate in the U.S. compared to the rest of the world. This means that if all goes well, there will be a great deal of available credit, which is helpful because government deficits are going to crowd the credit market fairly badly. It also means, however, that if things go wrong (that is, much worse inflation in the U.S. than in Western Europe), these deposits could all disappear in 90 days or so, and the ensuing credit problems would be horrendous.

We will now examine one of the reasons why the deposits will probably, for better or worse, stick around for some time.

PROBLEM 2
Government Spending

As you are reading this, the U.S. government will almost certainly be proposing to spend more money this year than it will receive in tax revenues. This prediction is based not on any partisan political assumptions but rather on the credit record of the U.S. since World War II. The difference between tax revenues and expenditures is made up by borrowing.

There is a great deal of moral and practical confusion about government debt. First, it is not necessarily wicked for a government to spend more than it collects in a given year; until recently, the main chunk of national debt was that incurred by World War II. Even the most righteous critics of government spending would have a difficult time arguing that the U.S. should have kept its budget balanced in 1944. Second, there is the question of to whom this money is owed. In general, the debt is financed by issuing obligations that are then bought by banks and insurance companies. This is a subtle point, because it means that government deficits amount to an income transfer from people who pay taxes but have no savings to people who have large amounts to deposit. Servicing the interest on the national debt means collecting tax revenues and paying them out to holders of government securities. The size of this transfer depends on the interest rate the government has to offer; thus there are all sorts of social and inflationary implications linked to one magic number, the prime rate.

This situation is not peculiar to the United States. Most Western economies, and Japan too, are finding that, politically, expenditures always have a constituency and budget cuts do not. The percentage of the GNP in these countries that will go to support nonworking population, that is, retirees, is going to grow fairly steadily over the next twenty years as a result of simple demographics. Either the retirement age gets pegged at eighty-five or the ratio of workers to nonworkers will drift steadily downwards toward one (this has essentially already happened in some countries).

The situation that is unique to the United States and that guarantees that government spending will be the major factor in credit markets for the life of this book is that no serious attempt is being made in America to control two of the principal cost burdens on the government, namely, medical expenses and military spending. Although some efforts have recently been put into law to control hospital expenses for Medicare patients per visit, these laws just fossilize the current costly rate structure and put no limit on the amount of money a given person can ultimately ring up as a government medical bill. The government is, in effect, obliged to buy services from physicians and hospitals, and the providers of the services are allowed to set their own price. This provides, one hopes, quality medical care, but at a price that is nothing less than staggering.

Military spending keeps increasing for the same reason: the Pentagon asks for certain weapons systems and is rarely denied them outright by Congress, and then these systems are purchased from suppliers who in practice can set any price they like for their services. This is a strong statement, but an examination of the cost history of any real, delivered weapon system since the mid-1960s shows, typically, that original cost estimates were highly unrealistic and that the systems contractors have an alarming tendency to need more and more money as a project proceeds.

Basically, as things are constituted at present, the federal government is obliged to pick up the tab for all sorts of purchases over whose price it has no control. A person retiring at age sixty-five can pretty much bill the government for twenty years' worth of the miracles of modern medicine. Likewise, the Army, Navy, and Air Force can each insist on their own typically overlapping sets of equipment from their own favorite contractors (the management of the contracting firms usually being heavily populated with former Army, Navy, and Air Force officers).

There is no reason to assume that this system will change for any reason short of total catastrophe. Thus it is safe to assume that financing of government deficits over the next decade will keep interest rates from dropping to the levels, around 4% to 5%, that were standard before the Vietnam War. It is also safe to assume that this level of borrowing will cramp business financing, at times severely, and will induce recessions of different intensities and duration. But that situation is, if you understand the implications, at least manageable; runaway inflation (that is, 100% or more) and total depression (25% permanent unemployment) are both situations that the government can avoid with relatively minor changes in policy.

PROBLEM 3
Energy

You may have noticed that, although it is a decade since the first "oil shock," most people depend on private gasoline-powered automobiles for transportation. Furthermore, Americans live in a country in which it is thought to be part of an "energy policy" to provide low-interest loans to elderly persons so that they can continue to blow hundreds of gallons of extra fuel oil out the smokestacks of their under-insulated residences. And as a final point, you are unlikely to be the owner of a solar-powered anything, except perhaps a calculator. We are not even going to address the problem of generation of electricity in nuclear power stations; construction costs have now made these economically impossible rather than politically impossible (and, believe us, economic is the highest grade of impossibility).

It is interesting watching energy matters come and go as news. There will be, for example, a news feature that Boeing has developed a new type of nonsilicon solar cell with great economic promise or that processing of amorphous silicon is progressing by leaps and bounds. Then, nothing is heard about these developments, and as this is written no products of significance have emerged. Do all these research breakthroughs go to some vast "elephant's graveyard" for old *Popular Science* topics?

For example, what became of the government-sponsored

Synfuels program, intended, among other things, to develop ways to process coal into liquid fuel? Other than repeated tales of scandal, corruption, and officials drawing magnificent salaries, there has been no Synfuels news in years. Think of all the experimental vehicles, running on ethyl alcohol, methyl alcohol, hydrogen, and propane, that have been presented to the curious public since the early 1970s. Gone, like the memory of a closet filled with paisley shirts.

The fact is, as soon as the gas lines disappeared and the price of crude oil softened, everyone in the United States quit being scared enough to demand any action on energy problems. It is not too much of an exaggeration to say that as long as there is enough gasoline for summer vacation and heating fuel for the winter, no one feels that there *is* a problem. Energy issues rank below even the boring matter of government deficits in opinion polls on public concerns.

The authors enjoy the curious experience of living in a small town in Northern California in which ardent countercultural faith in tiny, inefficient, and over-priced solar panels coexists with the mainstream belief that every American has an inalienable right to drive a 3-mile-per-gallon motor home towing a 20-gallon-per-hour speedboat. There is no point arguing theology, however, so we will proceed to the more pedestrian implications of all this.

There is ample reason to believe that petroleum prices are a powerful determinant of the inflation rate, because so many goods and services in daily life are dependent on energy costs. Furthermore, no matter how neatly things may seem to be flowing at any given time, the political arrangements and geology that underlie the world petroleum supply are quite treacherous. It happens, just to compound this, that the U.S. is no better prepared than it was in 1974 to deal with an oil shortage; in fact, it is in worse shape, because competing economies, notably Japan, are in a better position to bid for the available oil stocks.

Trouble in the Persian Gulf, trouble in Mexico, trouble in Indonesia, weather problems in the North Sea . . . any number of things can interrupt the oil flow to industrial countries. When this flow slows down, the price of oil will rise, resulting in an inflation pulse in the U.S. economy. It was just such a pulse that drove credit-card interest rates from 12% to 20% in the 1970s. The credit-card rates are still up there, and you

can be sure that a "temporary emergency" that would drive
inflation and interest rates up rapidly would have similar long-
lasting consequences.

PROBLEM 4
Technological Advances

A relatively easy way for you to assess the impact of new tech-
nologies on your own life is to see what economists predict
for job opportunities in the coming years. The usual prediction
is for a great number of jobs in the so-called service sector,
as opposed to manufacturing or farming. On closer inspection,
the service-sector categories that are to experience rapid
growth are fast-food workers, secretaries, building custodians,
and security guards. Has the development of massive computing power in tiny packages simply guaranteed you a future
cooking fries at McDonald's?

You, dear reader, probably have nothing to fear, because
the mere fact that you are reading this book implies that you
are an avant-garde techno-hipster with an admirable paranoia
about personal economics. It's everyone else that we are going
to worry about. The increasing technology content of products
and processes is squeezing middle-level jobs from the market,
leaving either largely unskilled work or highly technical work
as the remaining categories. This is an oversimplification, but
it correctly describes the direction of employment trends.

The reason this is worth keeping in mind is that many
investment schemes are predicated on the notion that you will
have smooth employment sailing for the next twenty years.
The whole idea behind IRAs is that you won't have to touch
your funds until you are ready to retire. Many real-estate
schemes require that you have a few hundred per month left
over to pump into your investment while you are waiting for
inflation to hand you some long-term capital gains. But it is
fairly realistic, if you have a high-paying white-collar job, to
expect to be fired, to be laid off, or to face otherwise dodgy
periods from time to time in the next decade. This is especially
true if you are part of a two-income family that depends critically on both paychecks. Upheaval in the employment market
makes this advice necessary: evaluate possible investments in
the light of what would happen if you had a severe income

reduction for three months. If it would force you to cash out of a situation at a loss, you are looking at imminent serious trouble.

A Model: As Easy as A, B, C

Once upon a time (the 1950s, to be specific), the United States was the only large economy on the face of the planet that had an intact manufacturing base and large amounts of managerial momentum. As recently as the late 1960s, European managers trembled at the thought of all-powerful American marketing and manufacturing know-how. Times have changed.

For simplicity, we consider only a few scenarios for the future of the U.S. Although America has in many ways a unique economic position in the world, so many different things have happened to so many different countries that there are potentially instructive comparisons to be made. We will summarize these possibilities by reference to three national cases; please understand that none of this is meant to be unflattering either to these countries or to the U.S.

FUTURE A
Low Inflation, High Interest Rates, Politics—Right

This combination of events would serve to make dollars a very expensive currency. Ultimately, the manufacturing base in the U.S. withers as a source of employment because of cheap imports, and all export earnings are derived from agriculture. This is whimsically labeled case *A* because of the social-structural comparison to Argentina. Although its inflation history is wildly different from ours, Argentina is basically a farm for the rest of the world, with the national wealth strongly concentrated in a small upper class that maintains its political position through severe repression. A situation in which unemployed auto workers could find jobs only as car-wash attendants could lead to all sorts of political shifts in practice, none of them very attractive. In a high-interest state the best return is on time deposits, and both stock markets and housing markets are depressed (tight money policies, if enforced severely, can produce deflation as opposed to inflation).

FUTURE B
High Inflation, High Interest Rates, Politics—Left

One response to the loss of competitiveness in manufacturing
is for workers to organize politically to protect their jobs. In
this case, labeled *B* for Belgium, it becomes practically impossible for businesses to fire people or otherwise reorganize; industrial inefficiency is underwritten by large-scale benefits
programs. The income distribution is much smoother than in
case *A*. The best sorts of investments in this economy are the
stocks of a few exceptionally well-run businesses and deposits
in the currency of other nations with lower inflation rates.
Although this case is politically quite democratic, there is
not much opportunity for large-scale innovation in economic
activities.

FUTURE C
Variable Inflation, Variable Interest Rates, Politics—Middle

In this case the inflation rate and interest rates are dragged
around by events in more dynamic economies. Strong regional
differences and ethnic-group politics prevent a long-term co-
herent political direction. The nation muddles through because
of great mineral and agricultural wealth. The *C* stands for
Canada. Every few years, the investment picture changes as
energy costs and balance of trade bring industries in and out
of favor. Inflation is not severe but it is neither readily predicta-
ble nor apparently affected by half-hearted government mea-
sures. The income distribution is reasonably democratic, and
the large resource base guarantees a certain amount of prosper-
ity, but the business climate is so dependent on external factors
that only firms with well-developed specialty niches make
money year after year.

Where Do We Go from Here?

The three situations outlined above are possible ways for the
U.S. to adapt to its somewhat less magnificent role in the world
economy. We also hope to have reminded you in this chapter
that the world banking system is in serious trouble (whenever
you hear bankers reassuring the public that everything is OK,

you know it's bad), that there is no substitute for petroleum on the immediate horizon, that government deficits won't be fixed by Christmas, and that the new high-tech job marketplace could find you in a uniform staring at a parking-lot TV monitor instead of designing circuits.

This is not necessarily personal bad news; it just means that if you let things drift they will get worse. You may safely figure that everything you know how to do is rapidly becoming obsolete information, but this just means that you are in for an adventure.

Learn how to do something else! If you are interested in stock-market investing, make an effort to read everything you can about a particular industry. And do your homework on the mechanics of stock trading. Why should you expect to walk into a brokerage office and have someone step forward and begin making money for you?

If you want to buy some modest rental property, find out how to do simple plumbing repairs and carpentry yourself. Everything you approach as an investment has within it a potentially more interesting experience than generating numbers in a bank account; for all you know you may find you like building maintenance better than your boring desk job. In any case, remember that money isn't really money—beyond the bare-necessity level it represents an opportunity to make something interesting happen. You can think of money and your investments as a way of expanding the universe of things you find interesting, and then you will be more likely to be happy yourself and to do something that is coincidentally socially useful. Because you can't take it with you, make sure you don't waste your life worrying about it.

INDEX